# Letters to and from an Innocent Man:

## How Lies and False Accusations Can Change a Man's Life

by Maria Moeller-Hackler and James Hackler III

RoseDog Books
PITTSBURGH, PENNSYLVANIA 15238

RoseDog Books
585 Alpha Drive
Pittsburgh, PA 15238
Visit our website at *www.rosedogbookstore.com*

ISBN: 978-1-6453-0445-6
eISBN: 978-1-6453-0467-8

# DEDICATION

This book is dedicated to my husband, Jimmy. He is my best friend, my lover, my protector, and the one person who has kept me grounded through all the bullshit over the past year. I love you, always and forever. Amen.

Your wife,
Ria

# TABLE OF CONTENTS

# Preface

I'm not really sure how to write a book or novel, but I'm going to give it my best shot and hope that whoever reads this can learn from our experience and see the signs of a corrupt judicial system.

My name is Maria Hackler, and my husband is James V. Hackler III, and this was our life from May 2016 to May 2017. It was one hell of a roller coaster ride that should never be ridden by anyone at any time. But first let me give you a little background on my and Jimmy's lives and how we met.

Jimmy and I met twenty-two years ago by a mutual friend named Selena. She called me on the phone and asked me to come over to her house because two of her friends were there helping her fix her car. So, I went to her house and that was where I met Tony and Jimmy (Tony was Jimmy's cousin). It wasn't love at first sight between Jimmy and me, but there was an instant connection that has lasted twenty-two years. We became friends first, and our relationship grew from there. We dated for a while, and then we went our separate ways for a few years.

The next few chapters are Jimmy's story, my story, and then our story and our letters. The letters themselves will show how mentally and emotional Jimmy gets for sitting in jail for eight months on lies and false accusations. I just hope that this book can help just one person, if not more, that truly innocent people can be found guilty on false accusations, lies, no evidence, and hearsay.

# CHAPTER 1: Jimmy's Story

Jimmy's story begins six months after we broke up in 1997. Jimmy got married to his first wife, and they had three children together. Their marriage lasted about six years, and they got divorced. After their divorce, neither of them had stable jobs or housing for their children. So, they lost custody of them, and they were all adopted out. This devastated Jimmy because he loved his children very much.

He managed to move on, and he got his CDL license and became a long-haul truck driver and did this for ten years. During the years of driving, he met his second wife, Theresa. She would go with Jimmy on his travels, and they both enjoyed the time they were together. They were married about two-three years when tragedy would strike for a second time for Jimmy. Theresa died of a heart attack in his truck. The loss of his wife devastated him for a second time.

Jimmy continued driving trucks, and a few months after Theresa passed away, he began talking to a woman named Kathy from an online dating website. She lived in Michigan, and that's where his nightmare began. Their relationship was rocky from the start. They would argue and fight (not physically), and it would get bad at times, but they also had some good times, too. A year after they started living together, Kathy found out she was pregnant with their first daughter together. Kathy already had one daughter from a previous relationship, and she was six years old.

Kathy gave birth to their daughter nine months later, and they named her Beth. Kathy and Jimmy's relationship was still pretty rocky. Kathy would kick him out of the house for weeks at a time and then let him back in. Jimmy was still driving trucks at this time, so he would be gone for three weeks at a time. When he was on the road, she would bitch at him for being gone so long, and when he was home, she would bitch at him for being home and drinking.

Then, sometime in 2011, Kathy found out that she was pregnant again with their second daughter, and they named her Hailey. Now, by this time, Jimmy had lost his license from a DUI and had one domestic violence charge for breaking a mirror. So, now he was out of work and home all the time, and his drinking got worse. Sometimes Kathy was buying him the alcohol that she would bitch at him for drinking.

Now it was 2012, and Kathy had caused him to get his second domestic violence charge. This is how he got it: Jimmy was at home, sitting on the couch, watching a movie. Kathy comes home from the store with a large bottle of liquor and a two-liter of coke. Jimmy tells her that he doesn't feel like drinking, and he continues to watch his movie. She goes over and sits next to him on the couch, takes the remote, and changes the channel that Jimmy was watching. Jimmy gets up, not saying a word to her, and goes to his computer. While he is on the computer, Kathy walks over and turns the computer off. (Can you see where this is going?)

By now Jimmy is aggravated and goes outside to smoke a cigarette to try to calm down. He goes back inside, and there is a drink made for him, sitting on the table. So, he's like, "Fuck it, I will have one drink." Kathy starts bitching at him because he is drinking, so naturally they start arguing. Then, to make matters worse, she takes the bottle of liquor and pours it down the kitchen sink drain. Jimmy is pissed, and he flips the table and walks out of the house. He sits on the porch, smokes another cigarette, and the cops pull up because Kathy called them once again on him.

Jimmy goes to jail again, and she had a PPO (personal protection order) placed against him. Kathy would later break that order several times by having Jimmy come to the house to babysit their two girls whenever she had to go somewhere. After a couple of weeks of this, Kathy takes Jimmy to the bus station and drops him off at night in -17-degree weather with nothing but his coat and suitcase. The bus station was closed, and she knew it would be.

Jimmy calls me on the phone, in tears, about 12:30 A.M. because he has nowhere to go and he is freezing. I asked him if he knew anyone close that would let him stay with them until the morning and then catch the bus that would bring him back to South Carolina. He said that he had a friend who lived a couple of blocks away, and I told him to go there to get out of the cold so he doesn't freeze to death. He went to Tony and Ann's house, and they allowed him stay the night.

The next morning, Kathy came and picked him up. As he got in her truck, the first thing that she says to him was, "You didn't die?" How callous was that? It was like she was expecting or hoping that he had died. During their relationship, she would degrade him in front of other people, especially her family, and they would join in. They would call him " an inbred sperm donor," a "southern inbred deadbeat," and "a cousin fucker," among other things. She was verbally, emotionally, and mentally abusive to him throughout their four-year relationship, and even after they broke up in 2012.

Well, Jimmy finally made it to South Carolina and found a job as a live-in maintenance worker at a hotel in North Charleston. He and I would talk on the phone almost every day. He was still in contact with Kathy, sending her money every week for their two girls. He paid for her car to be fixed and even bought her daughter a new charger for her scooter.

Kathy's daughter, Rose, was a piece of work, just like her mom. When Jimmy was living with them, she was allowed to walk around the house and call Jimmy an asshole and scream and yell at him, tell him that he is not her father, and that she didn't have to listen to him. Kathy wouldn't do anything about it but laugh and say, "That's my girl." I will never understand why Rose didn't like or respect Jimmy because he was nothing but nice to her, did things for her and with her, and he even bought her stuff that she wanted. He never mistreated her in any way. So, I guess that saying is true, "Children see and learn from their parents." Rose saw Kathy treating Jimmy like shit, and she figured that she could do him the same way and get away with it. I know a lot of people who are reading this are saying to themselves, "Why did he stay with her?" Well, it's simple: He wanted to be with his two girls, Beth and Hailey. He loved them very much and would endure whatever Kathy dished out just, so he could be with his girls.

Now, back to Jimmy living and working at the hotel. He was sending Kathy money, getting things fixed for her, and would send his girls cards and gift cards, but Kathy would send them back to him. This was the beginning of her cutting him out of Beth and Hailey's lives; this went on for months. Around the middle of May 2013, Kathy had told Jimmy that he could come back home to Michigan. So, he put in his two weeks' notice at the motel, trained someone else to take his place, and made preparations to go back home. The first week of June, he was ready to go home, and on the day, he was supposed to get on a bus, Kathy calls him and tells him that he can't come home, and she doesn't want him back. This is devastating news for Jimmy again because he was looking forward to going home to see his girls.

Jimmy has no job (she knows this), he has no money (she knows this, too), and he has one day left in the motel that he was living in and he has nowhere to go (she knows this as well). He is heartbroken because Kathy had led him to believe he was going home. Now he is homeless and broke. That's when he calls me again in tears because he didn't know what he was going to do or where he was going to go.

This is where our story begins: June 2013. But before I start our story, I am going to tell you a little bit about myself in the next chapter and how my life was before Jimmy and I were finally reunited after all those years apart.

# CHAPTER 2: Maria's Story

The year was 1995 when I met Jimmy, and in 1997, we went our separate ways. That same year I was going through my first hip replacement surgery at the age of twenty-seven and raising my son, Andrew, who was three years old at the time. This was my first hip surgery, but it wouldn't be my last one, either. I had had major back surgery just the year before, and I do not recommend it if you can help it.

I was in and out of a couple of bad relationships until 1999. That was when I met Chuck, who I thought was a decent guy...boy, was I wrong! Everything was okay for about a year when things started to change. First, I had my third back surgery in 2000, and that's when I noticed the change in Chuck. He started to become distant and not as supportive of me and the medical problems I was going through. But I kept telling myself that I was imagining things. Then, in 2001, I had to have a total right knee replacement. That was fun....not!

Chuck was fine for the first couple of weeks after my surgery. He would help me get in and out of bed, help me keep the house clean, and even helped with my physical therapy and took care of Andrew. That all changed about a month after my surgery. He started verbally abusing me, calling me names, getting angry for no reason, and even throwing things at me or near me. He even went as far as to throw me out of our apartment when I was still on crutches. But, like Jimmy, I stayed and gave Chuck the benefit of the doubt, again thinking that it was just too much for him to handle...his job, me, taking care of Andrew, and the house.

We stayed together for a few more years, then sometime in 2007, I noticed a really big change in his moods and behaviors. For instance, we would go grocery shopping, and when we got home, if the bread was smashed or crushed even just a little bit, he would flip the fuck out. He would scream and yell and blame me for it. I'd be like, "It's just bread, and you can still eat it." That would piss him off even more. It got to the point that Andrew and I were walking on eggshells around him because we didn't know from one day to the next what kind of mood he would be in.

I finally had had enough of his bullshit and told him that he needed to get help with his mood swings or he had to pack his shit and leave. He agreed to see someone, and the doctor he saw diagnosed him with Bipolar 1 with Psychotic Features. So, Chuck applied for disability because the doctor said he could not work, and I helped him through the process and paperwork because I went through it myself and knew how to fill all the forms out, all the appointments and the procedures he would have to go through. The process took two years for him to finally get approved for his disability.

Now, it was September 2009. Yes, ten years I was with Chuck and all his bullshit. I find out that he was sleeping with a girl that I thought was my best friend. That was the "straw that broke the camel's back." He had to go, and I needed to get back to some kind of normal life for me, my son, and my daughter, Jessica, who was living with me then. I needed to keep them safe and away from Chuck's sometimes volatile mood swings. They were and still are the most important people in my life, even though there was always this empty space in my heart that I could never fill and couldn't figure out why it was there.

Jimmy and I had been talking on and off over the years, but it was in August 2010 that we finally saw each other after many, many years. He came to Charleston to see his uncle for a week and he came to see me, too. As soon as he got out of his car, we hugged, and it was then that I realized that he was the one that filled that empty space in my heart. Our connection that night was so strong, that it had felt like no time had passed, and we had rekindled those old feelings again.

Jimmy was in town for a week, staying between his uncle's house and mine. It was the best week of my life, but like all good things, it came to an end. He called me when he was on his way back to Michigan. I thought my heart was going to break into a million pieces because I wanted him to stay with me forever. I begged him not to go back to Kathy and that rocky relationship that I knew he wasn't happy in. I had even asked him, in tears, to marry me because I knew that I could make him happy.

He told me that he couldn't stay because he needed to be with Beth, and he was still driving long-haul trucks. That empty space in my heart returned, and I didn't know when or if I would ever see him again. A whole year went by before I would see Jimmy again. We had talked on the phone whenever Kathy wasn't at home or when he was on the road, but it would hurt every time we would hang up the phone.

Then, the day after Thanksgiving 2011, Jimmy calls me and tells me to come to Columbia, South Carolina. He had a thirty-six-hour downtime, and he didn't want to sit there alone. I was so excited that I drove from Charleston to Columbia in one hour and forty-five minutes, and it normally is a two to two-and-a-half-hour drive. I met him at the truck stop, and as soon as I saw him, that empty space in my heart was filled once more. We spent the whole weekend together, and we had the best time. We stayed in a hotel, we drank, played games, made love several times, and just laid in the bed, holding each other like we didn't have a care in the world.

That weekend it was just me and him, and we completely shut out the rest of the world. Then Sunday came, and I could feel that empty space coming back because I knew that I would have to leave him in Columbia and not know when I would see him again. I cried when I left him, but we still talked on the phone, and that was some comfort just hearing his voice. It would be another year and seven months before I would see Jimmy again, and that was in June 2013. That was when he called me in tears and told me what Kathy had done. By this time, I was living in Florence, South Carolina, and he was still in Charleston. When he called me, I knew there was only one place he needed to be, and that was with me, and there was no way that I was ever going to lose him again. So, about 7:00 P.M., I borrowed my daughter's car and drove to Charleston to pick him up and bring him home with me.

As soon as we saw each other, that strong connection was still there, and we both could feel it. We went up to the motel room he had been staying in, and we talked for a long time. He told me about everything that happened between him and Kathy and some of the other things that she had said and done to him. I just couldn't believe that someone could be that vindictive and malicious. Boy, was I wrong! I would find out later just how bad she really was.

June 2013 is where our story begins and the struggles that we would have to endure, but we are still together and stronger than ever. There is nothing or no one that could ever break us apart.

# CHAPTER 3: Our Story

June 2013 was the beginning of a great and beautiful relationship, one that I always knew we would have. When Jimmy and I got back to Florence, he started working for my son's uncle doing construction. It wasn't a full-time job, but it was something.

Jimmy was still talking to Kathy, but it was mainly so he could talk to his girls, Beth and Hailey. This went on for about a month, then she changed her phone number, so he couldn't call his girls anymore. Kathy knew how to hurt Jimmy, and she would use those girls to do it.

Then, at the end of July 2013, we got the news that Jimmy's dad, Big Jimmy, had a stroke. His dad and stepmom, Rosalie, lived in Harriman, Tennessee. When we heard the news, we knew that we needed to go see him. So, on the first of August, we packed up my car and made the seven-hour drive to his sister's house in Harriman. We got to her house about nine that night and, needless to say, we were exhausted from the ride.

The next day was a Saturday, and that is a day that I will never forget. Jimmy, his sister, his nephew, and I went to see Big Jimmy. When we got there, Big Jimmy and Rosalie were sitting on their porch. Jimmy went running up to hug his dad and let out this yell like I have never heard before. That is when we found out that the stroke Big Jimmy had was the tip of the iceberg. Right after his stroke, while he was in the hospital, the doctors found a mass in his nasal cavity. It turned out to be cancer, and had they had to remove a third of his nose. We did not know about the cancer, so we were all in shock and Jimmy, was inconsolable for quite a while.

Finally, after Rosalie told Jimmy that the cancer can be operated on and he would have to have radiation treatments, but he would be fine, Jimmy calmed down. After all the chaos, we had a very good visit; they were soon laughing and telling stories from their younger years. The day started out bad, but it ended with smiles, hugs, and I love you's.

That night, when we got back to Jimmy's sister's house, we decided that this is where we should be to take care if Big Jimmy. So, within a couple of days, Jimmy had found a job at a warehouse, driving a forklift, and a month later, we had moved into our own apartment. We were doing good for a couple of months, but then in November another woman came into the picture, and Jimmy and I broke up for about five months.

I packed up my stuff and moved back to Charleston to be with my kids and grandbabies. There was also my dad who was not doing very well because he had Parkinson's disease. He was at the last stage of the disease, and he needed help getting up from his chair, eating, bathing, and getting in and out of bed. It was hard to see my father who once was a Marine for twenty-three years, in the community band, repaired wind instruments with his two, strong hands for twenty-five years, sitting in front of me, slowly slipping away, and there was nothing I could do to stop it.

Then in January 2014, I went to North Carolina to pick up my best friend of thirty-plus years, Cindy, and bring her and her family back to Charleston. We stayed in a motel until we found a place to live. I stayed with Cindy until March 29, when I went back to Tennessee because that empty space in my heart was telling that is where I am supposed to be. I left early that Friday morning and arrived back in Harriman about three that afternoon. Within an hour of me being back, I saw Jimmy and the other woman. Their relationship wasn't that great, either, and they ended their relationship, going their separate ways in April 2014.

I was back in Tennessee for two days when I got a phone call that would practically shatter my whole world. My son, Andrew, called me at 12:20 A.M on March 31 and told me that my father had passed away. My heart was broken and sad that he was gone, but I knew that he was no longer in pain or suffering anymore. A week later, I made that seven-hour drive back to Charleston for his funeral. The day we put my father's ashes in the ground was one of the hardest days of my life. I had lost other family members in the past: two sisters, two brothers-in-law, my only aunt, uncle, and a nephew in a ten-year span. I miss them all dearly, but losing my father was worse, and the pain of losing him was more than I could bear.

I went back to Tennessee after Dad's funeral and tried to put my life back together. I am thankful that Jimmy's sister let me stay with her until I got into my own apartment. Jimmy moved back in with her as well after his breakup with the other woman. We were not back together yet, and he was trying to keep his distance from me, but we were on speaking terms and that was about it. Then, at the end of May 2014, I finally moved into my own apartment. That is when Jimmy and I started to live together once again.

It started out that he didn't want me staying in my new place alone, so he slept on the couch for a couple of nights, and then he started sleeping in the same bed with me. Jimmy soon got another job at a different warehouse in July. He worked there until October, when I had to take him to the hospital because he was having chest pains, and he said he just wasn't feeling right. At the emergency room, the nurse took him right back and checked his blood pressure, and it was 186/201. The nurse put him right into a room, started IV fluids, and they used three nitroglycerine patches on him to bring his pressure down, but nothing was working. In the meantime, bloodwork was being done, x-rays were taken, and they did an EKG on him. When all was the testing was done, the doctor tells us that Jimmy had a mild stroke. He was only thirty-six years old at the time. That was hard to hear because I was still trying to get over losing my father just six months before, and Big Jimmy had his stroke just two years before, so I was scared of losing him, as well.

Finally, after hours of testing and IV fluids to get Jimmy stabilized, the doctor admitted him to the hospital to keep an eye on his blood pressure. He got into a room about seven the next morning; now we had been there in the ER since ten o'clock the night before. During the first day, his blood pressure was all over the place. He would be just sitting in the bed, and his blood pressure would shoot up for no reason. The doctors couldn't figure out why. On the second day, he was ordered to take a stress test, and he nearly passed out from that and his pressure shot up again. The doctors tried him on another medication that seemed to work, and his pressure started going down to a somewhat-safer reading. He was finally able to go home on the morning of the third day.

The night that Jimmy was admitted to the hospital, I called his supervisor at work and told him that Jimmy was in the hospital, but by the time Jimmy got out three days later, he had lost his job, even though he had all the paperwork from the hospital. So, now he was out of work again, and he started looking for another job when my car died on us. Here we are living in a small town with no car, and believe me when I say, "You have to have a car to get around or you're screwed." Lucky for us, there was a grocery store right behind our apartment. Walking there wasn't too bad, but walking back was. Jimmy would have to make several trips back and forth with groceries in hand. That walk was about the length of a football field, end zone to end zone. It was harder for me to walk it because I walked with a cane and couldn't walk long distances, but it had to be done so that we had food in the house.

No car and no job for Jimmy, and it was like that for about a year. Even though we were under each other's asses every day, 24/7, we enjoyed each other's company, we never ran out of things to talk about, and we never argued or fought about anything. We made do with what we had, and we were happy. August 2015 comes around and my son, Andrew, and his fiancé, Shay, needed a place to stay, so Jimmy told them to come stay with us until they can get back on their feet. Andrew and Shay made the seven-hour drive from Florence, South Carolina, with whatever they could pack in their car and moved in with us. By mid-September, both Andrew and Jimmy had jobs, and Shay was about two months pregnant with my fourth grandchild. My daughter has my first three grandbabies: Gemma, Noah, and Connor.

By the end of September, Big Jimmy had to have surgery again on his nose to remove any scar tissue and as much of the cancer that the doctor could get to. After surgery, the doctor told me and Rosalie that he had to remove more of Big Jimmy's nose and the cancer was deeper into his nasal cavity than he originally thought. The next step for him now after he healed from surgery was radiation treatment. The treatments began in mid-October, a couple of weeks after his surgery. By now, I was taking him to all his doctor appointments, CT or MRI scans, and any other appointments that he may have had. His treatments were set up for once a week for thirty-six weeks.

November and most of December came and went, and Big Jimmy's treatments were going well with no complications. It was Christmastime, and he had two weeks off from his treatments, so Andrew, Shay, and I decided to go to Charleston for Christmas. Jimmy couldn't go because he had to work and couldn't get the time off. This would be the first Christmas that we would not be together, and it wouldn't be our last. I went for the sole purpose to see my mother because she had been diagnosed with cancer just two weeks before. She would start her chemotherapy sometime after the New Year. We spent eleven days in Charleston and then returned to Tennessee.

Once we got back, life went back to its normal routine: Andrew and Jimmy working, Shay is four months pregnant, and I was taking Big Jimmy for his treatment and appointments. It was now 2016, and the roller coaster ride was about five months away. It's a ride that Jimmy and I did not volunteer for; we were forced into with lies and false accusations.

It's now February, and this was not a good month. Big Jimmy was just about done with his treatments, but on February 10, Jimmy calls me from work at 10:00 P.M. and tells me that I need to meet him at the hospital. As soon as Andrew got home from work, I drove to the hospital and meet Jimmy at the ER. The triage nurse took him right back and put him in a room. The doctor ordered x-rays of his knee to see what was going on; he was in so much pain and could barely walk. When the x-rays came back, the doctor couldn't really see anything, so he referred Jimmy to an orthopedic surgeon. Jimmy went to an orthopedic clinic in Oak Ridge, and the doctor sent him for an MRI on his knee. The news was not good at all. We found out that Jimmy had a torn ACL, and the Meniscus was shredded; he would need surgery to repair his knee. The doctor put him out of work for eight-twelve weeks, so he could have the surgery and have physical therapy. Surgery was scheduled for March 10, and he started therapy on March 15, going two-three times a week.

Jimmy was out of work during this time, but he had workman's comp paying him, so there was still money coming in the house, so bills could be paid. He was finally released to go back to work in May, and he was working for about a week when he blew out his knee again. By this time, my mother was going through her second round of chemo and doing okay, or so I thought. The doctor put Jimmy out of work for two weeks and could return to light duty, so he was switched from second shift to first, just so he could keep his job.

It was at this time when our nightmare would begin. A sheriff from the local police department came to our apartment and said that Jimmy needed to go talk to a Detective Franks. When Jimmy got off work, he walked to the station and talked to Det. Franks because he had no idea what was going on. He has had some devastating things happen to him in his life, but the news he would hear that day was the worst thing ever. Det. Franks told Jimmy that a detective from Michigan called and asked him to do a courtesy interview with him about allegations of molestation against Kathy's daughter, Rose, back in October 2008. Jimmy was shocked and confused about the accusations because he had not seen Kathy or Rose in four-and-a-half years.

Jimmy told Det. Franks that Kathy was doing this to him because he refused to sign his parental rights away to his two girls, Beth and Hailey. He showed the detective a message that Kathy had sent him on Facebook back in April 2014 demanding that he sign the papers when he gets them, but he never received any papers from her. Jimmy denied ever doing anything to Rose and just couldn't understand why Kathy and Rose were doing this to him. He even volunteered to take a polygraph test to prove that he was telling the truth. The test never happened because he was told because of his anxiety and blood pressure issues, that they could not morally and legally give him the test.

When Jimmy got home, he told me about the accusations coming from Kathy and Rose, and he was devastated and started to cry. He just couldn't believe that she would stoop so low as to accuse him of something so horrendous, just to get what she wanted…custody or their two girls. Now, I have known this man for twenty-two years, and I know what he is and is not capable of doing, and I know for a fact he would never hurt a child. He has known my children and grandchildren and has never hurt them in any way. He loves them as much as they love him, and he will tell anyone that Andrew and Jessica are his and those are his four grandbabies.

After his interview with the detective, we didn't hear anymore from Det. Franks or from Michigan. Our lives went back to normal, and Andrew, Shay, and their daughter, Lyric, moved into their own place, and I started taking Big Jimmy for his chemo treatments because there was a small mass deeper in his nasal cavity that the radiation did not get. These were done every Friday and would take about two-three hours each time, and they lasted from July to September 2.

It was a Friday when I took Big Jimmy for his last day of chemo, and when I got home, I knew there was something wrong with Jimmy. He had this glazed look in his eyes and was acting strange; he had been drinking, but he wasn't drunk. The look on his face was one that I had never seen before, and it concerned me. He kept asking me for the car keys, but I refused to give them to him. Well, he got them from me and threw them in the car and shut the door, but he didn't realize that he had accidentally locked the keys in the car. We didn't have the money to call a locksmith to come out and replace the locks and ignition on the car, so Jimmy took a bat and broke the driver's side window out. There were some neighbors outside watching him, thinking something else was going on they called the police. The police show up and run both of our names, and that's when we found out that Jimmy had a warrant from Michigan. Now, we had not heard a thing from anyone since back in May, and this was September. We just assumed the accusations were over and done with.

Jimmy went to jail that day, and his bail was set at $500,000 because of the warrant from Michigan. There was no way I was going to be able to come up with 10 percent of that. He sat in jail for a week before he went in front of the judge in Kingston, Tennessee. That's when we found out that he would be extradited to Michigan on the charge of Criminal Sexual Conduct with a child under the age of thirteen years of age, or CSC 2nd degree. This time I was devastated because that empty space in my heart returned, and I didn't know when or if Jimmy was going to come home. I talked to him on the phone, and I was able to see him once a week for an hour, but that wasn't the same as having him with me or having him next to me at night keeping me safe. Jimmy sat in the Kingston jail until September 28.

While Jimmy was in jail, Andrew, Shay, baby Lyric, and I went to Charleston to see my mother because she was not doing good, and the chemo did not work, and the cancer had spread to other parts of her body. She had nurses coming to her house to help her bathe and check on her meds and anything else she may need that my niece was unable to do. There was also someone from hospice coming in once a week to check on her, as well. She was still able to sit up in a chair but was sleeping in a hospital bed.

The visit with my mom was a good weekend, and she got to see baby Lyric for the first time, and that was a very special moment for both my mom and my son, Andrew. There was a lot of my family there at the house. My brother and sister-in-law were there from New Jersey, helping my niece take care of Mom. The weekend ended as quickly as it began, and we had to go back to Tennessee, that was Sunday, September 12, 2016. It was hard to leave because I knew that it was probably going to be the last time I would see my mother alive.

When I got home that evening, I walked into an empty house, and the reality of Jimmy still in jail hit me like a ton of bricks, and I broke down. A couple of days before I went to see my mom, Jimmy had gotten a letter in the mail from his employer saying that because he was a "no show" for three days, they were terminating his employment. I also had to cancel his second knee surgery that he was supposed to have on September 19. The hits just kept coming, and I was wanting everything to stop hitting us at once, but that wasn't going to stop anytime soon.

A week went by when I got that dreaded phone call from my niece at 5:30 A.M. on September 24 that my mother had passed away. I was again home alone because Jimmy's sister and nephew had decided the night before to go stay at their place and give me a break. So, here I am at my apartment, alone, with no one there for support. That morning is when I really needed Jimmy to help me get through the grief of now both of my parents being gone and not knowing how much more I can possibly take. When they say "the hits just keep coming," they weren't bullshitting!

The following weekend was my mother's funeral, but with Jimmy in jail and being extradited to Michigan on the 28th, I couldn't afford to go to Charleston for her services, and that hurt me to the core. That empty space in my heart was present again, and with everything that had happened over the past couple of weeks, it all came crashing down around me, and I just wanted to curl up in a ball somewhere and die! I didn't know how I was going to deal with everything, but I had to figure it out quickly. I had to start making plans to go to Michigan to be with Jimmy because I had promised him that he would not go through all this bullshit in Michigan alone. So, on Friday October 7, 2016, at 6:00 A.M., I left Tennessee and made the eighteen-hour drive to Michigan.

That was the longest drive of my life. I drove until I couldn't drive anymore. I finally stopped at a rest area, shut off the engine, locked the doors, and took a three-hour nap. I slept from 1:30 A.M. to 4:30 A.M. on Saturday, October 8. I still had about five hours more to drive before I got to Tony and Ann's house in Michigan. Tony and Ann are friends of Jimmy's, and they were going to let me stay in their house while Jimmy was going through all the legal shit. When I finally made it to their house, what was supposed to take eighteen hours ended up taking twenty-eight and a half hours because of the traffic in Chicago, and then an accident on the interstate two hours later didn't help; but instead made the drive even worse.

Tony and Ann came to the house the next day, which was Sunday, and took me out to eat and show me around town where the jail was that Jimmy was now in. His extradition from Tennessee to Michigan took a week and a half. I put money on his books, so he could call me. On Monday, October 10, Tony and Ann came back to the house and told me that they wanted me to come stay with them in their new house, which was about forty-five minutes away. They didn't want me staying in this house alone because they didn't trust Kathy if she found out that I was staying there alone. So, I packed up my car and they loaded a U-Haul truck with their belongings that were still in that house, and we made the forty-five-minute drive to their new house.

The next day was Tuesday, and I went to go see Jimmy at the jail. It wasn't face to face but through video-com; I have missed the physical contact with him. I had not been able to touch, hug, kiss, or have any physical contact with Jimmy since September 2, the day he was arrested, and it was now October 11. I would drive thirty minutes every Tuesday to see him for fifteen minutes from October 11, 2016, to May 16, 2017. I know fifteen minutes doesn't make sense to some people, but it was better than not seeing him at all.

Jimmy's first court appearance was November 8, 2016, for a Probable Cause Hearing. This was a hearing to determine if there was enough evidence to charge Jimmy with not one, but two, counts of CSC. Rose testified by video-com, and that was the first time in more than four years he had seen Rose or Kathy. Regardless of what was said or done during the hearing, the judge said there was enough evidence for the case to go to trial. After the hearing, I spoke to Jimmy's court-appointed attorney, Mr. Brown, and asked him if he believed that Jimmy was innocent and if he believed that Rose was being coached and taught what to say, and he replied yes to all three questions.

Rose's story had changed from the police report that was filed in May to the hearing in November and it became more elaborate. The charge for CSC first degree wasn't added until after Jimmy's warrant was signed in August; three months after the initial reports were done. His next court date was set for January 3, 2017; two more months he would have to sit in jail. Jimmy having to remain in jail meant that there were more things we were going to miss out on together. About mid-November, Tony and I drove down to Tennessee to get some of my and Jimmy's stuff out of our apartment. When we got there, there were things missing out of the apartment; some things we could replace, and other stuff we couldn't.

Our complete bedroom set was gone, all of our fishing gear, an Xbox system, some cookware, a Brett Favre jersey, two Green Bay hats, a T.V., and our vacuum were all gone. Jimmy and I had our suspicions on who could have done it, but we had no proof and no witnesses. So, we let it go and chalked it up to more things that we have already lost. Tony and I left the next morning to go back to Michigan. His SUV was packed with whatever we could get in it. So, here Jimmy and I are again with our whole lives packed in the back of an SUV, and there was so much that I had to leave behind, all because of lies and false accusations.

It was just about Thanksgiving…another holiday without Jimmy. Then we missed my son, Andrew, and Shay's wedding, and that was hard because he is my only son. Christmas 2016 came, and this holiday was the hardest because Jimmy is still in jail and this is the first Christmas without my mother. We would also miss out on Jimmy's birthday and New Year's Eve.

Before I begin with the year 2017, let me recap for you our 2016 year:

1. Jimmy blows out his knee at work in February.
2.) In March, he has surgery and starts physical therapy.
3.) My mom is going through her rounds of chemotherapy.
4.) Big Jimmy has to have surgery and starts his chemo in May.
5.) May is when Baby Lyric was born and when we find out about the accusations against Jimmy.
6.) June, July, and August come and go without any complications.
7.) September 2 is when Jimmy is arrested because of the warrant from Michigan.
8.) My mother passes away on September 24.
9.) September 28 Jimmy is extradited to Michigan.
10.) Jimmy finally arrives in Michigan on October 7, and it's the same day I leave to go to Michigan.
11.) We missed Thanksgiving and our son's wedding. There was also the

Probable Cause Hearing.

12.) We missed Christmas, Jimmy's birthday, and New Year's Eve together.

This was everything that happened to us in 2016, and the year 2017 starts off like shit. January 3 was the Preliminary Hearing where Jimmy enters his "NOT GUILTY" plea. Then we miss my birthday on January 6 and Valentine's Day in February. March 7 was the Pretrial Hearing and Motions, which all of the motions that the defense filed were denied. The next month is April, and that's when Jimmy's trial begins.

# CHAPTER 4: The Trial

April 4, 2017 was the day Jimmy's trial began. The trial began at 9:00 A.M. with jury selection and lasted until 3:30 P.M. that afternoon. After a fifteen-minute break, the prosecutor, Mr. Smith, gave his opening statement that took about thirty to forty-five minutes. Then the defense attorney, Mr. Brown, gave his opening statement that lasted about thirty minutes. The judge ended day one of the trial at 5:00 P.M.

April 5 starts day two of the trial. The first to testify was Rose (the supposed victim); she was on the stand for about an hour and a half. She did not act like a child that was about to testify about the most traumatic event that had happened to her. She got on the stand, smiling and giggling, like this whole ordeal was a big joke.

Mr. Smith starts by asking her to describe what happened to her in October 2008. She first tells how Jimmy made her watch a "dirty" movie, that now she knows was a pornographic movie. Mr. Smith then asks her how she knew it was pornographic, and she said that she had figured it out by herself later. She goes on to tell how she followed Jimmy down to the basement and that's where he pulls out a clear pink "dildo" out of a box that was on a shelf. They then go back upstairs to a room off the living room that she called "the office." That is where she says Jimmy touched her vagina with the "dildo," and he said to her that "it wouldn't fit." Rose says that is when Jimmy unbuttoned his pants and made her stroke his penis until he "ejaculated" in her hand. Mr. Smith asked her how she knows what the word "ejaculated" meant, and again she replied that she had figured it out later on her own.

Next, she says Jimmy went upstairs to use the bathroom, and she admitted that she followed him voluntarily upstairs and into the bathroom. She says that she asked Jimmy is she could hold his penis while he urinated. Rose then states that they both laid on the bed, completely naked, but nothing happened, and Jimmy never touched her. Then they got up and she got dressed, and while Jimmy was getting dressed, she asked him if she could see if they could both fit in his pants. She then says that Jimmy tells her "not to rat him out" to her mom. But as soon as Kathy comes home, Rose tells her about the "dirty" movie, but does not tell Kathy anything else that happened until eight years later.

Mr. Smith then asks Rose about seeing a counselor, and Mr. Brown objected to this line of questioning because the defense was denied access to her counseling records, but the judge allowed Mr. Smith to continue. Finally, the prosecution was done questioning Rose. It was Mr. Brown's turn to cross examine Rose, and before he gets his first question out, she blurts out, "My mom isn't coaching me on any of this." Mr. Brown asks her why she would say that, and she replied, " I don't know; she just isn't."

Mr. Brown was able to get Rose to admit that she was confused about certain events that had happened. Like the fact that her sister Beth had not been born yet but had told the CPS worker that Beth was around in 2008. Also, the fact that she was also confused about Jimmy being chased down the street by the police, when in fact that never happened. Mr. Brown asked her if she had ever told anyone else about the supposed molestation, and she admitted that she had told two of her friends about it months before she told her aunt, grandmother, and mom. He also asked her why she waited so long to tell anyone, and she said because she was scared of Jimmy. Mr. Brown was done questioning Rose, and she left the courtroom.

The next to testify for the prosecution was Rose's mom, Kathy. She testified how she and Jimmy met online and how their relationship was at the beginning. Then they started having problems, like arguing and fighting about everything. She also said that Jimmy contributed very little to the house, even though he was the only one working at the time. Mr. Smith asked Kathy if she had any adult toys in her house at the time, and she said that she did and that she kept them in her top dresser drawer. He then asked her if there would be any reason why a "dildo" would be in the basement. Kathy replied no and that she doesn't know why Rose would say that was where it was found. Then she made the remark that things were always getting moved around when Jimmy was living with her.

When Kathy was cross examined by Mr. Brown, he asked her if she had ever sent Jimmy a message on Facebook telling him to "sign the papers," referring to Jimmy signing his parental rights away, and she lied and said she never did. Mr. Brown then introduced into evidence a copy of the message, showing that she did send the message. He also got her to admit that she had called Jimmy "an inbred sperm donor," and she smirked when she admitted it and so did the jury. Kathy was finally done testifying, and the judge took a lunch break for about an hour.

After the lunch break, the prosecution's next witness was Detective Rias. He testified that Kathy had come into the police station the day after Mother's Day in May 2016 to file a report of Rose's claim against Jimmy. He also said that a couple of days later, Kathy brought Rose in to file her report. Det. Rias said he then turned the reports over to the CPS worker, and that was it. He also admitted that there were no interviews done with the aunt, grandmother, or the two friends Rose supposedly told, and no one else was ever looked at or questioned to see if someone else could have done these things to Rose. Kathy's live in boyfriend was never interviewed or even considered as a suspect.

Det. Rias also admitted that the warrant for Jimmy wasn't signed until August 2016…three months after the initial reports were taken. Det. Rias was the last witness for the prosecution. The CPS worker or Rose's current counselor was never called to testify. The prosecution rested, and now it was the defense's turn for them to present their case.

The one and only witness for the defense was Jimmy himself. He took the stand in the hopes that the jury would believe him and that he did not do what he was being accused of. Mr. Brown asked him if he ever molested Rose and Jimmy said "no," that he had never touched her in any way inappropriately. Mr. Brown asked other things like how he and Kathy had met, how was their relationship, and how long it had been since he had seen Kathy, Rose, Beth, and Hailey. Jimmy said it had been four and a half years since he had seen any of them.

Mr. Smith began to cross examine Jimmy; he asked him about his two domestic violence charges, and Jimmy admitted to breaking a mirror on one and flipped a table on the other charge. Mr. Smith then asked Jimmy how many children he had, and Jimmy said he had two with Kathy. The prosecutor brought up the three children that he had with his first wife. Mr. Smith didn't give Jimmy a chance to tell the jury that he no longer had custody of them and he had not seen them in twelve years. Jimmy was then asked if he was paying child support, and he replied that he wasn't but he was unable again to tell the jury that he had been in jail since September 2, 2016. Jimmy was done testifying, and he went back to the defense table and the defense rested their case.

The judge took a fifteen-minute break before closing arguments began. After the break, the prosecutor, Mr. Smith, began first by saying that either Jimmy or Rose were lying about their stories and that they both couldn't be telling the truth. He said that Jimmy was a bad father for not protecting Rose and for not paying his child support. He goes on to say that the prosecution didn't need any proof or corroborating evidence in this case because Rose's word was "good as gold," and that's all they needed.

Next, the defense attorney Mr. Brown gave his closing argument, and he said that he wouldn't call Rose a liar but that she was confused about certain events and embellished her story each time she told it, adding more details to make it more believable. He also brought the fact that there was no police investigation done and why weren't the aunt, grandmother, or Rose's two friends called to testify. He finished by saying that Jimmy was an innocent man and to find him guilty would be an injustice against his client; with that Mr. Brown was done. The prosecutor was allowed to give one, last statement. He used the only evidence that he had and that was a picture of Rose when she was six years old at the time of the supposed incident.

The judge then turned the case over to the jury, giving them the jury instructions at about 5:00 P.M. on April 5. The judge also told the jury that dinner had been brought in for them and that they were to eat without discussing the case; when they were done eating then they could start deliberating. They started their deliberations at 6:00 P.M. The waiting was the most nerve-wrecking time I have ever been through, and the waiting was even more unbearable for Jimmy.

The jury sent out their first question around 7:30 P.M., and they were asking for the transcripts from Rose's testimony. The judge informed them that it would take several hours to get her testimony typed and printed out. He then told them that they need to return to the jury room and use their notes and memory of her testimony and that they needed to come to a unanimous decision before they left that night. It was about ten minutes later that the jury sent out their second question; this time they just wanted a certain part of Rose's testimony. They wanted the part where Rose and Jimmy were in the office, what he did with the dildo, and if the act of penetration took place.

They received the transcripts and went back to deliberate, and within thirty minutes, they had reached a verdict. Everyone filed back into the courtroom to hear the verdict. The judge read the verdict as followed: As to count 1: CSC 1 with penetration…NOT GUILTY. As to count 2: CSC 2nd degree: GUILTY!

I was devastated, and I broke down in the courtroom; I just couldn't believe that the jury had found Jimmy guilty with no evidence, no witnesses, and a hearsay case full of inconsistences and lies. The jury was excused, and Jimmy was taken to the law library, right across the hall from the courtroom. The guards let me go in to see him. I hugged him and broke down again. He kept telling me to calm down, that he would be okay, and that he was more worried about me. I turned to the guards and made them promise me that nothing would happen to him in their jail.

It was about 9:00 P.M. when I finally left the courthouse. I was physically, emotionally, and mentally exhausted from the day's ordeal, and I still had a forty-five-minute drive back to Ewen that I had to still do. That was the longest day of our lives, and our whole world had just been turned upside down by one little word: GUILTY. The justice system had failed Jimmy in the biggest way, and he was now looking at a prison sentence for something he didn't do. False accusations, shoddy police work, and a vindictive woman has put him in this situation.

I have tried to remain strong and positive for Jimmy, but deep down I was falling apart. Sentencing was scheduled a week later for May 16, 2017 at 3:00 P.M. The fear of not knowing what prison he will end up at and not knowing when he will be back home with me was starting to set in. Jimmy does not deserve to be in jail or prison for something he didn't do. During the months of September 2016 to May 2017, Jimmy and I wrote numerous letters, poems, and songs to each other. We wrote about how much we love each other, how much we miss our life together, and how fucked up this whole case has been.

In all of the letters Jimmy wrote me, never once did he ever admit to molesting Rose. His story never changed…unlike Rose's story, which changed and became more elaborate and more things added each time she told it.

The next chapter are some of our letters, list of songs, poems, and some of the pictures that Jimmy drew for me. After you read them, I hope that you come to the same conclusion that we have…JIMMY IS TRULY INNOCENT! He was railroaded by a small town, "good ole' boys club" justice system.

# CHAPTER 5: Our Letters

Jimmy and I wrote many letters to each other, some of which are included in this book…not all of them, but some. There were many songs that were written for him, but I am just including a list of the songs and artists. I also sent him cards and some pictures, but the poems I wrote to him are.

Some of our letters will pull at your heart strings; some will make you laugh; and most all of them will leave you asking, "How could this happen to Jimmy?" These letters will also show what happens to someone's mental stability when they are wrongfully accused of something they did not do! I have retyped our letters because some of Jimmy's handwriting is hard to read, but everything is word for word from our letters.

All of our letters are not included because there are over one hundred between the two of us, and I don't want people to get bored. So, I have chosen the ones that I thought would give you an idea of some of the emotions that Jimmy and I were going through during our ordeal.

Just remember that these are our actual words, and nothing has been changed but a few names. Some spelling and punctuation isn't perfect, and some letters are longer than others, and some of the language is strong, so this book should not be read by children under eighteen years of age…readers be advised. The point is to read the letters and see what happens to a truly innocent man's emotional and mental stability when he is wrongfully accused, convicted, and imprisoned on lies and false accusations for something HE DID NOT DO!

September 12, 2016

Ria,

Hey baby girl, how are you doing? Well, I guess I did it good this time. As you know, Michigan is coming to get me. In a way, I'm glad, so I can get this dumb stuff behind me. I'm very sorry for my behavior toward you, and I love you very much. I'm not sure how it's going to turn out in MI, but I'm gonna fight it to the end. Sorry 'bout the handwriting, but the pens we get on commissary are like four inches long and flexible, so we can't stab each other. LOL. If you don't come to Michigan, I would understand. We still need our apartment here, along with our things and my job. I'm sure once I get up there, it's going to go pretty fast. Please see if Tony and Ann will bond me out and maybe let me stay with then till court is over and done. I'm scared and I feel so alone... I'm really confused and messed up right now. Why is Kathy doing this to me? I'm almost tempted to see if Tony can get Kathy to drop it all if I sign my rights away. After all, that's all she after anyhow. I'm a good person and don't bother her. If you want, stay here until it's time to come get me, I don't want us to lose everything we have on my account. I'm sure I'll be okay, but I know you and the always and forevers. LOL. I love you for not giving up on me, cause believe me, you're the first. If you haven't noticed, I decided to put Maria Hackler on the envelope just to see how it would look. Not bad, huh? Well, look at the bright side, if we are both in Michigan, it would be like a mini-vacation. The casino is about twelve miles from Bessemer. We just need to get out before the snow hits, or we will be screwed. Pack all of our winter clothes and some summer. We also need to get the car window fixed before you come up. This sucks. All I can do is sit and wait for only God knows how long. It's really not bothering me to not have a cigarette, but with the stress, it would be nice. I guess I'm going to need Tony's address and phone number. If I bond out up there, I'll need for him to vouch for me on somewhere to stay. Please, write me back, even when I'm up there. It's rough not knowing how you're doing or getting by. When you write back, will you put some of the pics of us from Graceland, so I'll have them to take with me to Michigan? I love you, Ria. I guess it's bye for now, but not forever.

Love Always and Forever, xoxoxo
Jim

P.S. Tell my sister I love her and miss her and for her to also write me whether I'm here or there.

September 12, 2016

My dearest love,

It was so hard for me to keep it together when I saw you in those chains. I wanted to run over to you and hug and kiss you because I miss your hugs and kisses so much that it hurts. The nights are even worse with you not next to me. You are my life, and you are not going to go through this shit in Michigan alone. I will sell everything I have to be with you up there. It is all material shit anyway; we can always buy stuff back later.

Tony said we could stay in his house in Ironwood if we need to. He also said that Mr. Brown would be the best public defender to get when you get to Michigan. Tony and Ann are pissed about this whole situation and that they would help in any way they can. The Packers won yesterday! It wasn't televised, but I was watching the scoreboard. I will let you know who wins AGT, too.

This should not be happening to you or us. You should be home with me where you belong. I will never understand how people can be so vindictive just to get what they want, but that's okay…Karma has a way of showing her pretty face when they least expect it.

I love you, baby, always and forever. You are my everything, and I will always be here for you. I just hope you realize just how much you mean to me and know that I am not complete, and I'm lost without you here with me. You keep asking me why I love you. It's because you keep me grounded and love me just the way I am. There's your answer.

I love you and miss you very much. Pa and I will write you again tomorrow.

Loving You Always & Forever,
RiRi


September 15, 2016

My love,

I'm sorry that I broke down when we saw you today. It's just that I miss you so much and am completely lost without you here with me. I have been kind of numb since Monday after court, then Kevin dying and then my mom's situation…when it rains it pours. I went and talked to Gary after I left you, and he sent me to first see Lt. Emitt at the jail about your surgery on Monday, but that was worthless because of the hold from Michigan. Then he sent me to see Freida at the court house about an emergency hearing about your surgery, but she said the same thing about the hold.

I called the attorney's office in Michigan, but Mr. Brown is out of the office until the end of September, but I left a message for his daughter to call me. I am trying everything I can to help you, but I feel like I'm not doing any good. I will never give up on you or us because we both deserve to be happy, and I will do whatever it takes to make that happen. I'm sorry that I won't be here this weekend to talk to you, but just know that I will think about you every minute of the day, and seeing you only once a week is driving me crazy.

I miss looking into your gorgeous, blue eyes, kissing your soft, sexy lips, and doing other things with you. (You know what I'm talking about...lol) I miss your hugs and your arms around me at night. I miss our fishing days together, I don't want to go without you. I am going to ask you one more time and if you say no, I won't ask you again.

WILL YOU MARRY ME? YES OR NO CIRCLE ONE

Loving you Always and Forever,
Ria


September 17, 2016


My beautiful Ri-Ri,


Well, it's Saturday, and I can't help but to think about how you're doing and how the visit is going in Charleston. We got commissary today. I got twenty packs of Kool-Aid, ten packs of Ramen noodles, one pack of fireballs, a t-shirt, pair of boxers, a pair of socks, and some Sweet and Low. Also, I got your letter with your pics today. I'm so blah without you. These pens they give us are crap. Well, Friday the 23rd will be the end of the ten-day hold, so I'm hoping they don't show up. If they are coming, then I wish they would hurry the hell up already. Every day I sit here is for nothing; just dead-time, which isn't fair. I can't wait for us to be back to-gether again. I was surprised when you said you missed hearing my music, lol. I didn't think that was possible. I'm trying to sleep as much as possible to make time go by quicker, but I'm starting to get sore. My back hurts, and I've got a bruise on my hip. Also, my knee is hurting bad from getting up and down outta bed. This place is so loud that I keep a constant headache. I feel like I'm in a zoo, lol. Baby, I know it's hard to do, but don't worry about me too much to where you worry yourself sick. I will be ok. No matter what happens, just remember. I love you now, always and forever!!!! I'm sure we will be back together soon; it's just a matter of time.

September 19, 2016

Hey, baby, how are you doing? Well, today's Monday, four days till my hold is up. With a little luck, they won't show up and just release me. I'm worried about you. I don't like that I'm not there to help with everything and you having to figure everything out on your own. I hope we are able to keep all of our stuff and the apartment. We were just starting to do ok. Well, I've definitely made up my mind, and I hope you approve and back up my decision. No matter the outcome, I think it will be best that I sign over my rights to the kids. I'm never going to get caught up on child support, and it's just going to end up causing me another problem. We are never going to be happy as long as Kathy is involved. I can't afford to live as it is and by me signing off I wouldn't be responsible for child support, so we would have more money. Life is changing and moving so fast, I'm not sure if that's good or bad, but we will manage to get through it together. I'm not sure how or what I did to deserve a woman like you, but I guess there's somebody watching over me to think I should be happy instead of being miserable the rest of my life. I know I'm not the best guy in the world and I have a lot of emotional, mental, and anger issues, but I'm going to try and work on them the best I can. We have a lot to talk about once I get out of this nightmare I'm caught up in. Tell my sister I love her and thank her for me for staying with you through all this madness. I LOVE AND MISS YOU SO MUCH!!!!! I think I'm starting to freak out, lol. I'm sick of being stuck with fifty-eight other fucktards. It smells like feet and ass in here. We get to go outside in the recreation yard for an hour a day, as long as the weather is ok. Thank God, cause it's the only means of some fresh air. I think I've read about eight books so far. I'm not too sociable and keep to myself as much as possible. I don't play cards or chess, and I don't wanna get caught up in long conversations with a bunch of meth, ice, and pillheads, which is why three-quarters of these people are here for. My days are so long, and my sleep schedule is way off. We get up at 4:30-5:00 A.M. for breakfast, then meds at 7:00 A.M., lunch is between 10:00-11:30, then dinner is between 6:00-8:00 P.M., and meds again at 9:00 P.M. Not to mention they do head count every three hours, and if we go outside, it's whenever the hell they feel like letting us out, lol. Most times I can keep it together, and other times, I feel like there's no end, and I get real depressed. Like now I'm just blah, I've slept so much I've got a headache, and my back and hips hurt from laying down so much on this metal ass rack with a gym mat not even a half-inch thick. I miss you and my bed. I try not to think about too much, so I don't get down, but there's not a lot to do except write letters, read, sleep, and watch T.V. But it's hard to watch T.V. cause they keep flipping channels, and they are so loud I can't hear the damn thing anyways. Well, baby, my hand is starting to cramp from writing, but I love you dearly and will keep in touch. I love you so, so, so, so, so, so much. xoxooxoxxoxox

Love Always and Forever,

Jim

P.S.: Well, now I'm really depressed. I just got off the phone with you, and as my luck would have it, I was going to call you back, but I have no calls left. So, now I'm out of a job, my attorney dropped me, I'm still sitting here for only God knows how long, and on top of everything else, I can't call home to talk to you. I feel like an utterly worthless loser! I've got such a bad headache, and I know my blood pressure is up, but, oh, well, it is what it is. Forget about calling Michigan anymore. If they're coming, then let 'em. If not, then fuck 'em. Just deal with TN from now on, ok. If I'm still here Friday, then I need you to call here about 4:00 P.M. to find out if they are going to release me or what. This is getting fucking ridiculous. I hate Kathy with all my being; this is such bullshit and very unfair. I have lost so much over bullshit lies that she had Rose cook up and then they're wanting to send me seven states away on allegations that happened seven year ago...WTF... I'm in such a bad, pissy mood, I could just scream. It's up to the D.A. and the judge to release me Friday. I hope they let me out. Well, hell, I'm going to sleep, I guess the only thing I haven't lost is you, but I'm sure that's next.

Love You Always.
Jim oxxoxoxoxo
Now my pen died...grrrrrrrrr


September 18, 2016

My love,

I love you and miss you very much. Its 9:38 P.M., and I am watching the Packers vs. Vikings, and I am missing you even more than usual because we would always watch the games together. I think seeing my mom this weekend helped me a lot, and I am feeling a little more comfortable that she will be leaving this world soon. I know she will be with my dad, in no more pain, or not have to go through anymore treatments. She has lived an incredible life for eighty-five years. She married the love of her life, had one child, and adopted six others. She has sixteen grandchildren and twenty-eight great-grands, and has seen them all. She has been pretty lucky to have seen all she has seen.

I am getting the window fixed this week, paying the car insurance, rent, loan payment, your phone calls, home and commissary money, and some groceries for the house, then the rest will be put up, along with the reimbursement check that comes in for when we have to go to Michigan. Then, on the first, I will pay rent again and the car payment. The cable might be shut off, so I will set up your phone calls to my cell phone. As long as I pay the rent every month, we will have a place to come home to. With no one here, we shouldn't have a light bill, so I will have enough to pay rent and the car payment. I will just have to figure out how to get insurance paid.

I hope you come home soon because it just isn't the same here without you. I miss you so much it hurts. Yes, Maria Hackler does look pretty good…lol. It's very easy to write as well…lol. When I say always and forever, I mean always and forever; you're stuck with me, baby. I am going to say bye for now, but not forever.

Loving You Always & Forever,
Maria Hackler

September 22, 2016

My dearest love,

It was good seeing and talking to you today. You are not a loser, and I am not going anywhere; I am here to stay. What I am writing to you is how I feel, and nothing or no one will ever change the way I feel.

<u>I LOVE YOU</u>

"I love you" means that I accept you for the person that you are, and that I do not wish to change you into someone else. It means that I will love you and stand by you, even though the worst of times. It means loving you even when you're in a bad mood or too tired to do the things I want to do. It means loving you when you're down, not just when you're fun to be with. "I love you" means that I know your deepest secrets and don't judge you for them, asking in return that you do not judge me for mine. It means that I care enough to fight for what we have, and that I love you enough not to let go. It means thinking of you, dreaming of you, wanting and needing you constantly, and hoping you feel the same about me.

That is the unconditional love I have for you; the same unconditional love that I have tried to explain to you over and over again. If you ever have any doubts or start feeling down, just read this letter again and again until you have no doubts about my love for you. I have told you for the longest time that you and I are meant to be together, that we have a very strong and special relationship like no one else. I know that you tried to fight it and tried to run me off, but you have to admit that we belong together, and we have a very special connection that cannot be denied.

You are my world; you keep me grounded. You are the reason I get up in the morning and enjoy going to bed at night, knowing you are beside me to hold me tight. I am going to say it again…" I AM NOT GOING ANY WHERE, I AM WITH YOU FOREVER & ALWAYS!!!!! We will get through this together and be stronger together, because we can get through anything and show her that she didn't break either one of us down or apart. She probably thinks that I am going to leave you because of all this shit she is putting you through, but she just doesn't know me that well, does she?

I love you and miss you very much and can't wait for you to come home to me and we can be happy together forever. We deserve to be happy.

Loving You Always & Forever
Ri-Ri

September 27, 2016

My dearest Ria,

How are you doing, baby? I'm okay, I guess. I'm so ready for all this to be done. I guess this week is going to be the tell-tell of it all. Either way I'll be out of here this week, either by transport, or they'll let me go Monday. I love and miss you so much. I just wish we could get back to normal. I'm sorry I won't be out to attend your mom's funeral. I'm not sure if you're going, but I understand if you do, just be careful. I'm just trying to take it day by day, but it seems like the days are getting longer no matter how much I try to sleep it away. This is probably going to be the longest week since I've been here. There are two Hackler's in here, so every time a guard comes in and yells "Hacker!", my heart skips a beat and my stomach twists in knots thinking the worst. I'm trying to keep my head clear and stay positive, but it's been challenging to not think about it. I miss everything: our fishing trips, our joking and laughs, our baths together, but most of all, your smile, eyes, and your voice, along with your kisses and hugs. I really hope things go ok without any problems this week. I tell ya, this is a screwed-up jail to be in. This place is so over-crowed. Some people are sleeping on the floor with just a blanket. It's only 3:00 P.M. and dragging ass. Well, just woke from a slight nap and now it's 4:55 P.M., lol. Woo hoo, another hour down...lmao!!! Well, so far so good; I think I will make it through this Tuesday, only to find out how Wednesday's going to be. I'm listening to the news in the background, and they say the cold is starting to set in. I guess this Thursday is going to be 68 degrees for the high. I hope I'm out of this crap and home before winter hits. What are we going to do about Xmas this year? I really want a real tree this year with better ornaments, especially with Andrew, Shay, and Lyric being here, but I don't know if they are going to Charleston this year. Well, I just got off the phone with you, and I'm glad you got the check, so you can get the car window fixed. It really was enlightening to hear your voice tonight; I miss it so much. I scheduled a visit for you and Cindy for 8:00 A.M. on Thursday. I reckon the neighborhood will be about normal since Heather got served eviction notice. Which is a good thing. If you want will you get another cheap chair for the front chair for the front porch, so we can enjoy the few sunsets we can before it turns cold. I can't wait to get back home. I need a long bath, cigarette, Pepsi, my own clothes and, of course sex, lmao. Well, now it's 10:00 P.M...lol. I just got outta the shower; it was actually nice and hot tonight. This will be the last letter I write while I'm here in Roane County. If I'm transported, I'll continue to write from there, but this is my last envelope I have, so it is what it is. I love you so much, and you are always in my thoughts.

Loving Always and Forever,
Jim xoxoxoxoxoxo

September 28, 2016

Dearest Ri-Ri,

Well it's Wednesday at 10:30 A.M., and my nerves are shot. Every time the door opens, my heart skips a beat and my stomach drops into knots. So far so good. I just hope I can keep riding it out till Friday. I can feel my pulse all over my body, and my blood pressure is off the wall, on top of a headache. I hate this whole not knowing stuff. I swear, when I see you, I'm going to just hold you for a long while. I miss your cute, soft smile, see-through blue eyes, and your warm touch. I don't like the fact you're out there without me and suffering over this stupid shit. I'm glad I talked you into paying the cable, so you won't be bored. No matter what happens, I guess I'll figure it out. I feel a little better knowing you're standing by me and not abandoning me like most would do. I guess what doesn't kill us will make us stronger. I got your card today, but it was just a Xerox copy. It was a very beautiful card. Thank you, baby, I feel the same way and love you very much, too. Thanks for not leaving me on the back burner, as Jessica put it. I mean, wow, I thought she cared for me more than, that but I guess not. Still hurts my feelings, though. Well, tomorrow is Thursday, and I hope it goes by fast and peaceful, without any problems and no sign of MI or anyone else. Two more days till Friday, swing through Sat-Sun, then it'll be Monday.

(This letter was never finished because he was transported to Michigan)

October 9, 2016

Hi, baby,

Well, you finally got me to Michigan—ha ha. Not how it was originally planned, but I'm here for you. Saturday was hell, but I got through it. Friday was even worse; the drive up here was crazy. It was fine until I hit Chicago, then it went downhill from there. I was stuck in 4:00 P.M. traffic for three hours (remind me never to do that again). Then about two hours later, I was stuck in traffic again because of a car fire, and it took one and a half hours to go just five miles. By then I was done driving and found a rest area and slept for about three and a half to four hours. Woke up about 4:00 A.M. and drove the last five hours, got to Ironwood about 9:30-10:00 A.M. on Saturday morning.

I met Tony, Ann and Katie today...they are great!!! They have been so nice and are so willing to help us in any way they can. When they got here to the house, Ann comes in with new pillows and sheets for the bed; she had already bought a couple of towels, hand towels, and wash clothes. Then, without warning, she and Tony hand me $100 for anything else I might need, so that's how I was able to put money on your books.

When she handed me that money, I broke down and cried because I was going to use the last $27 I had to put on your books, so you could call me. Those two are your true friends, especially if they are letting me stay in their house and give me money, so I can get what I need or do what needs to be done. They are truly remarkable people.

I love and miss you so much that it hurts. I can't wait for the day when I have you home with me and back in my arms, where you belong. I LOVE YOU ALWAYS & FOREVER...AMEN!!!!!

Love ya, baby,
Ri-Ri Hackler

October 31, 2016

Hello, baby,

I love you very much. I am so sorry that things didn't go the way we were hoping and you couldn't come home with me. I really believe that Mr. Brown will do a good job and find you innocent and you will be able to come home. I am still trying to figure out a way to get back down to Harriman to get our stuff, and I have been asking any and everybody I know to go to the house and pack it up and put it into storage unit, just so we don't lose everything, but I guess you know how well that is going…not!!!

Don't ask me what I did to piss your sister off because I have no clue. When I talked to her on the phone, she was at our apartment cooking dinner for her, Shannon, Robbie and Christina, then she was going to clean up the kitchen and go back to her apartment, so they can get all of their shit and leave to go back to SC on Tuesday morning.

I don't see how your DV charge from years ago has any relevance to this case at all and that being one of the reasons you couldn't come home; it's bullshit, this whole case is bull-shit. I am really worried about you because when I saw you today, it looks like you haven't slept in a month, and I worry that you're not eating enough because you are trading your food for coffee. I am going to try to put some money on your books. Hopefully, if Sue buys our bedroom set and sends me the money, I can put $60-$70 in your account.

I just wish they would let you have other things besides socks and underwear. I know I am probably just rambling on about stupid shit, but it's the only way I have to really communicate with you. Those fifteen-minute visits on Tuesdays and the few minutes that we talk on the phone just isn't enough.

I guess what I'm saying is…I miss you, all of you not just bits and pieces, but everything about you. I miss your smile, your laugh, the way you would kiss me on my forehead or come in the kitchen and hug me just because. I miss going to bed at night and waking up in the morning knowing you are right beside me. I miss the things we would do together, the fishing, yard sales, the flea market, or just staying at home… I MISS IT ALL!!!!!!

We will get everything back like we had it, maybe even better. I keep thinking that maybe this whole situation is a test of how strong our relationship really is: the honesty, loyalty, devotion, and how strong our love is for each other and if we can survive this test, then we can survive anything… TOGETHER FOREVER.

I love you, babe, with my whole heart and from the deepest part of my soul, there is no one else for me but you; don't ever doubt my love for you. I will write you again in a couple of days, if not sooner.

I Love You Always & Forever,
Maria Hackler
For now & always your wife


November 6, 2016

Hello, Pa,

I have missed calling you that and thought maybe that would put a little smile on your face. I know how much you love music and I think this is the perfect song for us right now, just bits and pieces.

SEE YOU AGAIN
It's been a long day without you, my friend.
And I'll tell you all about it when I see you again
We've come a long way from where we began

I'll tell you all about it when I see you again.
First you both go out your way
And the vibe is feeling strong
And what's small turns to a friendship
A friendship turns to a bond
And that bond will never get lost
The line will never be crossed
Established it on our own.

You and I have been through rough times in our lives, but we have always managed to find each other for emotional and moral support. Now I am asking you to lean on me because I know you are mentally and emotionally exhausted and feel like you have no more fight left in you. Let me fight for you because she can't manipulate or intimidate me with her bullshit. Put all of your trust in our hands; when I say ours, I mean mine, Mr. Brown, Tony and Ann's. Let us take all of the burden and you just sit back and focus on keeping yourself healthy as much as possible.

You cannot—and I mean CANNOT—give up because I need you in my life to keep me from going insane and not bring out the whole "Southern Attitude" that could get my mouth in a whole lot of trouble. You keep me grounded and focused on what needs to get done out here.

I love you very much and miss you even more. I know you are depressed and your anxiety level is very high, and you think that this nightmare will never end, but I promise you it will end soon. Please, please, please don't ever give up on us or give up hope because then she wins, and I will not let her defeat you or me with her craziness.

I know I probably sound like a broken record telling you over and over again that this whole case is bullshit and to never give up, but I have to keep saying it to you until you start believing it yourself. If you give up, then all of this fighting would be for nothing.

The Social Security office is sending papers for you to sign, so I can finish filing out that app online. When I get them, I will bring them up there for you to sign. Once you get out of there, I am going to try to get you into the mental health clinic to get you some counselling because I know you are going to need to talk to someone and be put on some meds to help you cope with all of this shit going on. I'm sure I will need something, as well, because I am emotionally drained and there are some days that I am a basket case and all I can do is cry.

I am trying to make these letters longer for you, but I don't want them to be too depressing for you. Here is something to make you smile...Katie is a trip, she is a chatterbox, and I can just see you and her having conversations about everything under the sun. She keeps me laughing at some of the things she says and does. She is so funny, she keeps me busy when she gets home from school. I have been helping with her homework every day; it should only take about twenty-thirty minutes, but it turns into one-two hours because she loves to talk. She reminds me of Morgan; she is a trip.

Well, I am going to go for now, but not forever. I will write again on Wednesday, unless by some chance you are coming home, and then I will show you just how much I have missed you... (hint, hint, wink, wink) Ha ha, made you smile!!!

I Love You Very Much!!!

Always & Forever,
Ria

November 6, 2016

My love and best friend, Ria,

Baby, I think I'm on the verge of a mental breakdown. I'm so stressed out, I'm profusely sweating in my palms. I constantly shake, and my head is constantly aching with pressure. I'm definitely going to need some professional help when this is all over. All there's to do in here is think, and it's getting the best of me. I think about my mom and how she died, Theresa and how she died, my dad going through his cancer and how he is and will be, and how it will all end for me. My nerves are a wreck. Depression, stress, and anxiety are eating at me 24/7, and I can't do anything about it. I'm not sleeping to well; every time I close my eyes, I see everyone I love and miss so much, and wake up sweating and on the verge of crying, but I hold back. I need my sleep meds. I stay up until I practically have to sleep. I think a lot about how this is Kathy's hometown and how she has so many people and influence here, and me being an outsider and having only a couple of people to help me in this. Baby, I do and always will love you. I should have just listened to her and signed my rights away when she told me to, then none of this would be happening. She was right when she said I'd be sorry and my signature wouldn't be necessary. She has had this planned the whole time. She has the money, the pull, and knows all the right influential people to get what she wants, and I'm not sure Brown is going to be enough to prove what she is doing, especially with Rias on her side. I understand I've got past domestic violence charges and the brandishing a firearm charges for a damn BB gun, but this is an all-time low for even them to do this to me. I've never been in such a position to feel the way I do. When me and Kathy split up, I never wanted to step foot back in this state ever again. I knew if I fought her for visitation, she would make my life a living hell, so I left her alone and have said and done nothing in four and a half years. Now, all of a sudden, she wants it her way one more time. I hate to tell you this, but if she pulls this outta her ass and wins, well, she will win 100% because I'm not going to give her the pleasure of making me go through life behind bars and portrayed for something I'm not. I'm going to ride this out until the end, but I'm doing everything I can just to endure the sixty-plus days I've been in jail now. I won't and can't imagine doing a long period for something I did not do.

I'm developing some very serious psychological issues in here and don't know how to handle them or what to do. I'm not a suicidal person, but I refuse to let her win. Not like this. I don't wanna die, but I won't live life the way she wants it. Being in here isn't doing me any good against my case, and she knows it. I wish there was some way I could get Brown to somehow get me out of here. I swear, I don't know how they can hold me without a reasonable bond. I don't understand how it's all based on hearsay and character witnesses. She has a lot more character witnesses than I do, and that's not fair when I'm not even from here. I need out, so I can defend myself. I feel so helpless…like a sitting duck just waiting to be shot. Now I know why people always say the system is broken and unjust…because it is. I didn't understand the probable cause hearing. How do they determine cause from hearsay? Whatever happened to innocent until proven guilty? I feel like I'm being targeted and set-up for failure. How much longer is this madness going to go on? I never touched that girl and now I wish I never got this tattoo on my chest for Kathy. This should've never been allowed to go this far. I never thought people could have somebody's life changed so quick. Am I even getting fair hearings? Why wasn't there an investigation? Why didn't Rias contact me when we were talking to the detective in TN? I don't understand a lot, even the detectives in TN thought it was b/s.

I'm the one that hunted the TN detectives down. I was doing everything to resolve this. Now I've lost my house, job, our things, and everything we knew as our life. I don't know what to do about my knee; it hurts, I know that. We don't have any money for me to keep calling, and that's really got me down because I miss our long talks. Baby, I'm scared and don't know what to do. These walls are getting to me. I know I probably rambling over the same shit, but I'm going nuts in here. It sucks watching people get released for serious drug charges, and I don't even have a chance of posting bond. I've got to lay down. I love you, Ri-Ri. I hope bond gets lowered soon.

Love, Jim


November 9, 2016


My one and only Love,

I love and miss you very much. I miss our long conversations we used to have and the times that we would just veg-out in the bed, watching T.V. together. I especially miss our all-nighters together. We will have some serious making up for the lost time sessions when you come home!!!

I finished that app for Social Security today and sent those forms back that you signed on Tuesday. Not sure how long it will take to get an answer from them; probably a couple of months. I probably already told you that you have been approved for Medicaid.

I am trying to come up with the money for your bond to get you out. I wish our car was paid off because I would get a title loan on it to pay that 10 percent. I would have gotten you out weeks ago if I could have. That's a lot of money when we don't have any. I talked to Tony about getting a loan on the motorcycle, and he said that (1), those title loans are shady, and (2), he would have to talk it over with Ann and see what she has to say about it.

It felt so good to hug you on Tuesday and give you a kiss. I didn't want to let you go. I wanted so bad to bring you home with me that I almost started to cry when I had to let you go not knowing when I was going to be able to hold you again. God, I hate that all this shit is happening to you, me, and to us!!

After all of this is done and you are found not guilty, I think you need to fight for visitation with Beth and Hailey. You deserve the right to have a relationship with them, whether she likes it or not. You are their father and signing your rights away will never change that.

I know you can't do anything about that now, but it is something to seriously think about doing when all of this other bullshit is over and done with. You are a good person, and those girls need to know their father is a kind and very loving dad.

Both Jessica and Andrew called today to see how you are, and I told them what has been going on, and both of them agree that this whole situation is bullshit and that they love and miss you very much.


November 10, 2016

Hello, baby,


I am sorry that I broke down on the phone with you. I try to stay strong, but sometimes I just can't hold my tears in. Some days are better than others, and today was not a good day; come to think of it, I haven't had a good day since Sept. 2 when all of this started.

Tony and Ann try to keep me in good spirits, and I try

to put on a happy face, but the night time is when it is the worst because you are not with me filling that empty side of the bed where you should be. Okay, that's enough depressing shit, on to something else!!

Tomorrow night I will be hiding out in my room because Katie is having two friends spending the night, so I am sure it is going to be loud with three little girls running around the house. So, I will be watching movies on my tablet most of the night or until I fall asleep. I guess I am not used to being around kids; it has been a while since I have been around kids Katie's age. It's all good, though.

I just hope that the people interested in the couch and bedroom set don't back out on getting them because I could really use that money to put on your books, gas, cigs, and anything else that I might need to get or pay for. I am going to get the most important things from the apartment and anything else that I can stuff in the car. Going to try to bring our dishes, pot and pans, silverware, and our fishing gear and our deep fryer back up here.

Please stop saying that you're sorry for putting me through this. This is not your fault; this is not your doing!!! Kathy has done this to us; she is the reason that we have lost everything that we have worked so hard to get and pay off. We are a team, we are soulmates, and we will get through this together, like we have done everything else…TO-GETHER!!!

It was nice to hear your voice again tonight, but I love hearing your voice all the time. I miss that, I just you period, I will not feel completely whole again until I have you back in my arms. I am trying to make my letters longer for you to read, so maybe the time goes by quicker. Gives you something to do, so you're not so bored. I have re-read your letters several times already.

I love and miss you so much and can't wait until you come home, even though it might be here in Michigan for a little while. I will write you again on Sunday and will see you on Tuesday.

Loving You Always & Forever,
Ri-Ri
(Mrs. Hackler)


November 8, 2016

Hey, baby,

Well, today didn't turn out so well. When I got to hug and kiss you, I didn't want to let you go. Honey, we've got to come up with the bond money or I sit here until Jan. 3. I know you tell me not to worry about you or anything else in here, but that's all I can do is worry. I love and miss you so much.


November 10, 2016

Hey, honey,

I just got off the phone with you, and I'm sorry you were crying. I guess I have no choice but sit here until Jan. 3, 2017. I don't wanna miss the holidays with you, and I'm so sorry I won't be there with you for Thanksgiving, Xmas, and we can't even have our New Year's kiss. All I can do is sit here in my crate like a good dog. I tell ya, it sucks having to eat, shit, piss, watch T.V., shower, and sleep all in one room with three or four other people and never know what's going to happen minute to minute. Just like a kennel, I'm locked up in a fuck-ing animal shelter with no hope of finding my owner…lol. I just want it over. I don't understand why my lawyer isn't even trying to get me out since there is nothing to make these charges stick, except hearsay. No facts, witnesses, proof, nothing. What I think is it's all a conspiracy and Brown is part of it, knowing my luck which is "0." I'm just over it. They can only beat on me for so long. It has to end sooner or later, I would imagine. If we can't get the bond money, maybe we can come up with enough to hire a different lawyer to get me out. I don't think Brown is even trying; that's what's got me worried the most. If he knows, this is b/s and they have nothing like he says, then why isn't he pushing for my release? I've watched enough crime shows to know most paid lawyers would have me out until trial. Why would he have me sit for four months on a b/s case. I'm sorry for rambling. I love and miss you more than life itself. We had five people in my cell, but I got out last Friday and I got out today. The one that got out today was a pretty cool guy. He was fifty-six years old, and this was his first time in. He was here for two and a half weeks for kicking a box and breaking a broom, so the state of MI put a DV on him. He went to court today, and they gave him an OR bond. It was bittersweet; I'm glad he got out, but he was my chatting buddy. He looked and reminded me so much of my dad. He also had cancer; he just went to his doctor appointment the other day at Grandview and, sadly, they gave him three-five years to live. While he was here, we became good friends. We were both older, so we related well. We sat up every night just talking, while the other two younger folks stayed up watching dumb-ass Adult Swim. I kept him supplied with coffee, and we would just chew the fat about life. Now I'm back to myself; before he left he gave me the couple of things he had left from commissary, which is a jumbo honeybun and two bags of crunchy Cheetos. He knew I didn't get commissary last week and I rat hole everything in order to keep coffee. I still have about one quarter of a bag left out of the three bags I bought two weeks ago, but it's not going to last too long, so I rathole and trade off different shit to get by. You're going to laugh, but I've accumulated a lot since I've been here. Right now, as far as food, I've got…two apples, two oranges, a sandwich baggie full of mustard packets, two jumbo honeybuns, two bags of crunchy Cheetos, two granola bars, two packs of cookies, one oatmeal cream pie, one apple pie, one bag of buffalo chicken flavored pretzels, one bag of oven baked Cheetos, four packs of single-serve drink mixes, and an old peanut butter jar one-quarter full of coffee…lol. Clothes I have the pack of socks and underwear you got me, plus a thermal shirt, four pairs of long socks, which I don't wear lol, and another pair of long socks that was given to me. I took one of the long socks and made a blindfold with it, to help me sleep when the lights are on and the other as a wash rag. I've even got dishes…lol. I've managed to get a bowl with a locking lid to save food if I choose to, a coffee cup, a tumbler cup w/lid, and two empty peanut butter jars with lids. One I use as a drinking cup and the other to store my coffee in, and a spork. I keep all my things under my bunk in a paper grocery bag. I also have a pair of foam earplugs, two pencils, six sheets of paper (as of now, lol) and seven stamped envelopes. I know you probably don't know what to think or you may even be laughing but in here, and to me, it's a lot and all I've got. They definitely break you down. When I got here, all I had was my deodorant and my tumbler cup and soap dish that I brought with me. When I was placed in a cell, I was issued a gym mat for my bunk, a towel, a blanket, a hygiene pack that includes one small container of deodorant, and a bar of bath soap (the size of hotel soap). There's not anything to do except watch T.V. or play cards, and the days are repetitive. I start my day by taking my meds (b/p & naproxen) at 5:00 A.M. I go back to sleep until breakfast @ 7:00 A.M. I then lay back down until lunch @ 12:00 P.M., and after lunch, I call you. I either read a book or lay on my bunk and watch T.V. until dinner @ 5:00 P.M., and after dinner, I call you again. Then again, I lay down watch T.V., read or play cards till lights out, which is usually between 9:00 and 10:00 P.M., depending on the guard, at which time I lay back down till I go to sleep. Every day is friggin' groundhog's day, except Tuesdays, when I get to see you for visits. Oh, I forgot, they issued me a sheet for my mat and a very thin pillow and pillowcase. I got inventive, though, lol, and I'm sure you'll smile on this one, lol. I took two rolls of toilet paper and put them inside my pillowcase and folded it over to sleep on. We get clean clothes on Fridays, clean sheets, towel and pillowcase on Saturdays, and are allowed to send out personals (socks and underwear) to be washed Saturday evening and get them back sometime Sunday, and that's only if you have a laundry bag issued to you. Thankfully, I do. If you don't then you wash out your personals in the shower with you after you're done washing your ass, lol. Which I did also the first couple weeks I was here. The shower here is small, and we use a trial size plastic baby powder container as a shower head. In order to heat water up in the sink, we jam an empty shampoo bottle between the edge of the sink and the hot water button cause it's a push button and doesn't stay on by itself. In my cell, there is four bunks, one shower, a toilet w/a sink attached to the top of it, and a metal picnic table and, of course, a phone on the wall and a T.V. At night the lights are only dimmed, never out. That's why I made a blindfold to sleep. Well, baby, I'll write again soon. I love and miss you very much. I wouldn't wish this on anyone; it sucks. I'm glad you've never experienced this, and I hope never do.

Love You So Much Baby
* Remember they read incoming mail

November 14, 2016

Hey, Ri-Ri,

How are you doing, honey? Good, I hope. I worry so much about you, but I know you are okay cause you are staying with really great people. I can't wait to get out and hold you tight. I'm really hoping Brown gets the transcripts by the end of the month and is able to get me back in court sooner to file the motions and get me out of here. I wonder what motions he's going to file? What are motions anyway, and what do they do? I also don't understand why it's taking so long. Jan. 3 is a long time in jail for a purpose hearing. What exactly is an all-purpose hearing anyway? lol I know I'm fuckin' clueless when it comes to all this, but I know you can google it for me and write me back with answers. I'm happy for you that you are getting to go to a dentist. I need one, too; since I've been here, I've lost a filling, broke a tooth, and my two bottom teeth are real loose, and my gums are deteriorating. If any part of being here is okay, it would be you getting to a dentist. I have my good days and my bad days, but I'm hanging in there, I guess. I'm okay until my anxiety kicks in, then it's all I can do to get through an hour.

It sucks not knowing anything for certain except for Jan. 3. I'm trying to write you positive letters instead of depressing ones all of the time. I really hope you have a good Thanksgiving, and I'm sorry I can't be there with you; don't give up hope, honey. I need you to still try to come up with bond money, so when he does get me a lower bond, we will have it. I wish we could have more time to talk on the phone. There's so much I'd like to talk to you about, but I forget half of it by the time I call. I know you was wondering about the extradition trip, so I guess here it is...I left Tennessee on Sept. 28, we went to Nashville, then Alabama, Florida, Georgia, South Carolina, back to Georgia, Mississippi, Alabama,

Arkansas, back to Tennessee, Kentucky, Virginia, W. Virginia, back through Kentucky, Indiana, Illinois, Wisconsin, and then here. I spent four days in the holding cell inn Searcy, Arkansas, and it was awful. I just want to come home, where ever that is, as long as we are together. We should save up and buy either an RV or a truck with a travel trailer. I don't know about you, but I'm tired of starting over and losing everything. My anxiety is getting the best of me, and I want outta here.

November 15, 2016

Hello, baby,

Well, another day of this shit jail. I'm hoping you get a hold of Brown, and he can get me in court sooner. Well, I just got off the phone with Cindy, and it was good to hear her voice, but now I'm a little down and out. This whole year has been shit between my knee, my job, this shit, losing our apartment, my sister, Shay & Drew, having to go back to SC. It's just all a lot to take in. I can't do anything about any of it. I can't walk it off or talk to anyone about it. All I can do is sit here and stare at the wall, and I'm over it. I want my life and entire family back. Please, please, please, baby, get me out of here!! Let Tony and Ann know exactly how serious and bad this is affecting me mentally, and I need the fuck out of here. I shouldn't have to sit here over the holidays. I feel like fucking screaming to the top of my lungs and punching the wall until it's over, but I can't. When is this shit going to be over? I'm sorry my letters are always depressing, but I'm going nuts in here. I feel like a trapped dog. I try to sleep but you can only lay down so long before everything hurts & I have fucked up dreams. I love you, baby, and I know this will be over one day, but when is that going to be?

I'm so blah, and I know my letters are downers and repetitive, and I'm sorry for that, but I don't know what else to do or think. I have a hamster that's constantly running as fast as he can on his wheel. We just got commissary and for $10, I got soap for $1 and a small bag of fireballs for $1.25. I'm glad it's Tuesday cause I get to see you tonight. All I have to look forward to is Tuesday visit, commissary, and Walking Dead on Sunday. Well, other than Jan. 3 and hoping maybe I'll get into court sooner. I'm doing a fucking stupid countdown, so now I've got forty-nine days till court. Baby, do you have any suggestions on my anxiety? I try sleeping, reading, watching T.V., playing cards, writing you, and talking to you on the phone, but it seems like nothing works. Sometimes it's so bad my lips, fingers, and toes tingle. I lay down, close my eyes, and pray it'll all end. It's got to all end, right? I love you, Ria, and I'm sure we will make it through all this, but this waiting game really sucks. Whatever happened to innocent until proven guilty and the right to a fast and speedy trial? I think the fast and speedy trial thing only pertains to people that are actually guilty, which I'm far from and everyone knows it, and even though my charges are what they are, I'm still innocent, and they have nothing, but they still keep me caged up, which I think is very unjust.

Well, its 3:30 P.M., and I'm just hoping time goes by pretty quickly, so I can see you tonight. I wish I could be put in a coma until I go to court. It would make things so much easier for me. Make sure when you go get our stuff that you get your Keurig and tray I bought you and the Xmas stuff from my dad. I think I'm going to be sick of coffee for a while when I get out, but I miss your sweet tea and seasoned potatoes. I know it's good to have time to think and reflect on life, but this is ridiculous. Instead I think about life, about Tennessee, my dad, us, and my sister. What's my dad's address, so I can write him? I don't know what I'd do or how I would feel if something happened to him while I'm in here. Wow, four months I'll never get back. I wish we could smoke in here; that might keep my anxiety down a little, instead of treating us like a zoo animal. I'm also so sick of the History & Discovery channels. I'm tired of watching Cops, Another 48, which I know you like that show and dumb-ass Adult Swim, Family Guy & American Dad. There should be a classification process to jail. They should keep the younger people together and us older folks that are calm together. Well, I talked to my sister and got her address, so I can write her, too. Like now, all of a sudden, my anxiety is kicking in, and I don't like this feeling, my friggin' knee is killing me. I don't know why, but it's been popping in and out a lot today, and it hurts bad, so I've been trying to stay off of it. I know I get to see you in a couple of hours, but I miss you so much and I just hate my life right now. Brown is going to have to do something to get me outta here, and I mean soon cause I don't know if I can do another month and half of this shit. He could get me in front of the judge for a bond hearing if he really wanted to, but I'm not sure if he's buying time or just don't give a shit, cause he's already free. Does he even care? I'm not sure if he cares or not, but it's affecting me in ways unimaginable, and I'm over it. Will I ever be released? Or will I ever get a lower bond? Why would it take so long for him to get the facts together? Am I being sentenced for a crime I didn't do and he's on their side? Am I going crazy? I don't know what to do or think anymore; my life is in his hands, and I don't even know what his strategy is or why he's waiting so long to ask the judge to at least give me a reasonable bond. I've been locked up since Sept. 2; isn't seventy-seven days enough for at least a lower bond? I mean WTF, is going on? Is he just letting me sit as long as possible and then just going to give up on me? Baby, what do I do or think? All I got to get in contact with my lawyer is you, and I'm starting to think he's even starting to beat around the bush and avoid you, too. This is such bullshit; any other state would've done had this figured out and done. I would be able to deal with all of this a lot better if I was at least out and with you. This is just so confusing to me. Why nothing is being done to get me out of here? Not meaning you, I mean my lawyer. Isn't there a limitation on how long they can hold me without a reasonable bond or proving a case against me? My lawyer and even TN detectives said they have nothing, so why the fuck am I being held so long? Do I have a certain amount of time I have to do? Brown said they have no experience with cases like this and they shouldn't have even brought me back here, and also, if there was anyone he was more confident winning against in court, it would be this Smith guy, so why the hell is he doing nothing? Are they friends and discuss things out of court over golf & a glass of brandy? It isn't so much that I don't trust him, I just don't trust the system or courts. The system is broken, and people get the shaft everyday cause of a make-believe trial and the judge and lawyers are in on it. In the report, Kathy mentioned that something happened with me in Indiana, but she didn't know what cause I never talked about it. Well, the only things that happened was Theresa's death and the stuff with Chrissy. That's where we lost the kids for being unfit. I'm wondering if Kathy is trying to get in contact with her? This is all b/s, I want nothing to do with this broke-ass county or this shitty state. Why don't they at least give me a chance to bond out and help prove my innocence? To make things worse, all the Xmas commercials are on, and that gets me every time. Please, get me out of here. I know you're trying, but I guess you would be the same way if it was you. I'm freaking out and don't know what to do. I know they are taking their sweet old time and don't care one bit about me. I remember you telling me that Brown told you they are waiting on me to crack, what does that mean? I'm not guilty of anything, what do they expect for me to do? I want this shit over, but I'm not playing along with their game when I've done nothing. I'm caught up in Kathy's twisted shit and don't know what to do, except sit against the wall and deal with it as best as possible, which is not working out to well.

So, you just left from our visit, and I'm sorry it didn't go so well, and you left upset. It wasn't my intentions, and I'm very sorry. I love you so much, but I have no one to talk to about all that's going on and how I feel. I have people around me, but I have no one around that won't judge me anyways. When you write letters, why don't you write on the front and back? lol. Well, I guess this letter has gotten long enough. I'm going to try and sleep. Remember, I love you so much, and although I can't be physically with you, I will still always be with you no matter what.

Love Always Your Husband,
Jimmy


November 15, 2016

To my husband,

I love you and miss you so much that it hurts. This letter is going to be some poems that I found, and I hope that you like them and whenever you are feeling down and feeling lost, read them again just so you know how much I love you!!

1.) My Only Love
Just to say I love you
never seems enough.
I've said it so many times
I am afraid you won't understand
What I really mean when I say it.
How can so much feeling,
so much adoration possibly fit into
those three little words.

But until I find some other
way of saying what I feel, then
"I love you" will have to do.
So, no matter how many times I say it,
never take it lightly, for you are my life,
and my only love.
I love you now more
than ever before.


2.) My Love
There are days when I lie awake in my
bed and wonder
How could I have gotten so lucky
You came into my life like those princes
of tales yonder
And made my life feel so complete
So now that I have you for myself, I
know for sure
That I am yours forever more.


3.) Have I Told You
Have I told you yet…
How much you mean to me…
Have I told you yet
about all the happiness you bring!
Have I told you yet
that you mean the world to me!
Just in case I haven't…
I want you to know that
You're the best thing
that's ever happened to me!
 I Love You


4.) Be Strong Babe
Yes, I have been through it,

our situations are similar,
they're different just a bit.
Tides of time are testing us,
we do not ever bow down
yes, we will be strong babe.
We're together & we'll be so forever.


5.) No Title
It's your smile,
it gets to me every time.
It speaks to me,
it tells me that you're mine.
It's your smile,
it warms my heart
and brightens my day.
I'll bask in it always,
if I have my way.
Have I mentioned,
you have my attention,
with your vibrant style,
that makes me smile.
I am so interested,
and invested
in this thing,
that's more than a fling.
I can't wait to see,
where it leads.
This wonderful ride,
that's you and me.


6.) No Title
To the world you might
be just one person
But to me...you are the world.

7.) You
Thank you for giving your heart to me
and trusting me with yours.
Thank you for walking beside me
and for wanting me at your side.
Thank you for thinking of me
and for always staying on my mind.
Thank you for making me smile
and for smiling along with me.
Thank you for being who you are
and for helping me be me.
Thank you for each day
and night,
and for always....
I love you

8.) My True Love and Devotion
They say, "The Older the Violin,
the sweeter the music." Well, I
see that in you, I see that in our love.
My love for you gets sweeter
and sweeter each day and so
are we.
Throughout the years we've
been together, it amazes me to
find more reasons to love and
cherish you. I tried to make a
list but I'm out of words.
My heart is full of joy and all I
know is...."I am not whole
without you."
For as long as I live, I cannot
think of the best gift but "My
True Love and Devotion" to you.
I Love You Now and Always.

9.) Untitled
Love is not just about
calling each other all day.
Love is about adjusting
and making way.
Love is not just about
walking in the rain.
Love is about
sharing the pain.
Love is not just about
sending messages and tweets.
Love is about
making each other's lives complete.
All these facts about love
are totally true.
Which I realized
when I fell in love with you.


10.) Love
Love...
bears all things,
hopes all things,
endures all things....
Love Never Fails


11.) Better Part of Me
The way you speak so softly,
the way you say my name;
the tender way you touch me,
I'll never be the same.
No one has ever moved me, to give my heart completely;
the part I held so tightly to,
you took from me so sweetly.
You move me like no other,
there just aren't words to describe;

the way your heart has touched mine,
and the way I feel inside.
The times that I am with you,
are when I feel so whole;
you are my anchor in life's storm.

12.) Don't Quit
When things go wrong, as they sometimes will,
when the roads you're trudging seem all uphill,
when the funds are low and debts are high,
and you want to smile but you have to sigh,
when care is pressing you down quite a bit,
rest if you must, but don't quit.
For life is queer with its twists and turns,
as every one of us sometimes learns,
and many a failure runs about,
when we might have won if we'd stuck it out.
Don't give up though the pace seems slow,
you may succeed with another blow.
Often the goal is nearer than,
it seems to a faint and faltering man,
often the struggle has given up,
when he might have captured the victor's cup;
and he learned to late when the night came down,
how close he was to the golden crown.
Success is just failure turned inside out,
the silver tint of the clouds of doubt,
and you never can tell how close you are,
it may be near when it seems so far.
So, stick to the fight when you're hardest hit,
it's when things seem worst that you
MUST NOT QUIT!!

13.) Husband
Mere words cannot begin,

to tell you how I feel.
You're the one thing in my life,
I can count on to be real.
We've had our ups and downs,
but whenever we're apart,
I still get an empty feeling,
deep inside my heart.
We've stood the test of time,
we've walked the narrow road,
and at the end of every day
it's you I want to hold.
I'm proud to be your wife,
I'm proud to be your friend,
and if given the choice,
I'd do it all again.

Well, I think thirteen poems should be enough...lol. If these don't tell you how much I love you, I guess I will find more to send to you. I love you baby...always have and I always will!!!

Love Your Wife & Best Friend,
Ri-Ri


November 19, 2016

Hey, baby, how are you doing?

I'm bored as hell, so I thought I'd come up with some funny, made-up poems to at least get you to smile or at least laugh. So here it goes...
"Sitting here, while the clock tick-tocks,
I stare at all I own in a bag and box.
I see I have nothing, neither here or there,
Just a few pairs of socks and some underwear."

"With nothing to do but sit and stare,
All I smell is nuts and butts in the shitty air.
But as I think of you and I start to smile,
Because I know we are only apart for a little while."

"Being without you really blows,
Thinking of how you're doing when it snows.
I know you can't drive really good in this shit,
So, I know on Tuesdays you're throwing a fit."

"So, when you're feeling down, and miss your other half,
Just remember I'm here thinking of you,
To make sure you still laugh."

I'm sure you're smiling & laughing now…LOL!!!!


December 5, 2016

Hello, Ri-Ri,

Green Bay won their game last night! Okay, I was thinking about my Xmas list, and the chances of me getting any of it are as about as good as me getting out of here before Jan. 3 cause we are broke and will be till I get out and get a job, but here it goes anyway, lol!!
My Xmas/birthday wish list…
NOTHING…
It's pointless to make a list cause I won't be home, we have no money, and it's just another day. I know that was probably not what you wanted to hear, but there is no reason for wishful thinking. I've done a lot of wishful thinking since all this started and absolutely nothing is being done about nothing. So, why keep it going? I'm just going to try to sit here the next thirty days and do the only thing I can

do...nothing.

Just sit, sleep, eat, and shit, lol. What a life, I tell ya. I do hope you have a good Xmas, though. I'm sorry I can't be there with you, believe me, if we had money, I would be. My b-day is just another day, but if I can, I'll call ya right before midnight for New Year's!!! Besides, I need you to hold your check you get at the end of the December until after court Jan. 3 because I'm sure we are going to need it. I'm sure they aren't going to let me out without some sort of cash bond. You need to save as much money up between now and then, please. I'm not sure they will lower it to $500, so we need as much as possible, and I hope maybe Tony and Ann could possibly pitch in a little, too, since the holidays will be over. I'm hoping it'll be a lot lower since I've been in here for a while. I don't think they are counting the thirty days I sat in TN or the bus ride here. I think they started counting my days from when I got here on Oct.7, which I don't think is fair, so if you could check into that for me, I'd really be grateful. I'm sure Brown would know, I guess. I believe I got arrested Sept. 2, so if they count it, Sept. 2 to Jan. 2 is five months, I think. Hell, I'm not even sure, four or five. I just hope I'm able to come home on the 3rd. I've never been so aggravated in my life. I want to know what motions he's filing, what bond amount he's trying for, and what he thinks the outcome of all this is going to be. At least what he thinks will happen on the 3rd and does he feel confident for me to get out on the 3rd. I need you to find out all of this stuff for me, please. I don't mean to be a pain in the ass, but you have a better chance of finding all of this out. You said they get us a Green Bay bed set; that's awesome. Do we still have our flannel sheet set, and what about our bamboo pillow? I know Andrew and Shay had one of them. I hope they are doing okay. I'll call them when I get out, if I ever get out. I think what I can't stand the most is the not being able to bond out and not knowing at all when I'll get out. I've seen so many people come and go;

hell, I'd post $20,000 to get out. They come in a week or two, go to court and are usually out the same day or within a couple weeks with time served. That one guy I told you about, come back for pissing dirty is already out. He was only in for a seventy-two-hour hold. I've been in for months and don't stand a chance at ever knowing for sure what the hell is going on. It's starting to seem hopeless. I know it's a change of subject, but next Sunday, Dec. 11, is the mid-season finale of the *Walking Dead*. I know you haven't been able to keep up with it, so we will have to catch up on it together, among all our other shows. Don't forget America's Got Talent is doing a Christmas special with all the previous people Dec. 19 @ 8:00 P.M. on the ABC Family Channel 48. I wish we could've been watching all of the Xmas specials together. Ria, there has got to be an end to all this, doesn't it? I just want to know when, this is all bullshit and has totally been way drawn out over her lies. This thing has given me a totally new outlook on life. I'm not going to be the same ole' me for a long time. I used to be so lively and friendly and would help anyone, but now I think it would be best to just keep to myself.

I believe the less people I know and deal with, the better off I'll be. I know I'm going to work on saving money a lot better then what I have done in the past cause this is bullshit that I'm still sitting here, and no one to help me. I have always helped everyone. Tomorrow is visitation, but I don't blame you if you don't show up cause of the weather. I've been trying to keep our phone calls short and sweet, so the phone card will last longer, and we don't have to waste so much money. I just asked for another one, so now I think I can get one more. I'll try to make it last all month, if I can. I love and miss you. I'm glad you're okay and keeping in good spirits with Ann and all. I'm sure it helps pass time and keeps your mind off all this. I'm sure it's a lot easier for you to get through this since you can go out to stores and for a drive and such. It sucks for me cause I'm stuck in my fucking 20 x

20 dog crate. Also, don't mail any more books here; some guards will let me get them and some won't cause they sell puzzle books on commissary. So, if you do get me anything, just bring it with you when you come for visit, to make sure I can have it. I know you probably hate getting my letters by now, I know I'm repetitive, but it's all I have to do. I've been listening to everyone's stories in here, and I'm not sure what to think. I've never had any felonies; the worst on my shit is my DUI and a few DV charges that were dropped. I feel I'm in here for murder or some shit. I guess Jan. 3 will tell the outcome for a lot of stuff, as far as what's being pushed, dropped, and if I can come home. I'm sure the one charge that carries life will be dropped.

Well, it seems as if it would anyways, don't you think? I don't see how they can charge me with this shit; all I know is I've got three and a half weeks left till we find out. I hope I come home; it's been too long since I held you. I love seeing you on Tuesdays, but it isn't the same. I need some fresh air and some real sunlight; the windows in here are the size of a brick. They use the warped privacy glass and are mostly covered, so hardly any real sunlight gets in. I'm sick of fluorescent lights and being stuck with nasty smelling ass people all the time. No privacy at all; we all eat, shit, sleep, and shower in the open, around each other 24/7. I need a hot bath, my Axe body wash, and a damn washcloth with my own clothes afterward. Grrr…three and a half more weeks. I hope we got money to get me out then. Please, save your check and everything in between that you can, so we have at least something to work with. Will you bring a pack of Marlboro smooths and a can or 20 oz. cherry Pepsi with you on Jan. 3, just in case? As far as the third goes, is it just for motions? I mean, I don't have to say anything, do I? I get out I think it's going to take a little bit to get back to my old self, but I'll try. This has been a very detrimental experience that I never want to go through ever again. I've been in jail and court and have been nervous but okay. This time is a lot different and worse cause the charges, they are trying to give me are felonies, 1 is fifteen years and the other is life. I'm scared as hell and don't know how I got in this situation. Well, other than Kathy trying to destroy me for custody. I don't know what to do or even what I can do to even defend myself, and that scares me. Also, it's frightening that this case and my life is in the hands of a man that doesn't know me, nor do I know him. The whole character witness thing isn't fair cause all the people I know here are somehow related to her, whether its family or friends, and that isn't fair. Why wait till now to pull some shit like this? I haven't heard shit from them in four and a half till she wanted full custody. I'm hoping Brown can show and make the judge see what all this really is. But, like I said, knowing my luck this is one big conspiracy, and they are all on her side.


December 6, 2016

Hey, baby,

I'm glad you was able to come see me today! Nice jacket!! lol... I'm miss your smile and talking to you so much. I was a little worried cause of the weather. I'm sorry you got stuck at Tony's with the arguing and such. Once I get out and get a job, maybe we can get an efficiency or something until we can get in something better and more secure. I was asking the guys in here, and they said there are one and two-bed-room efficiencies all around starting at $300 or so. I'm going to stay here long enough to do what I got to do, save up some money, then it's back south for us. I'm not comfortable, nor do I want to be up here any longer than we have to. We just don't belong up here; by the grace of God we was made in the south!!!

With me working, the casinos, and saving every penny, we can. Don't get bent outta shape…lol. When I say casino, I mean a limit of like $20-$40 a week; kinda like the lottery. Speaking of lottery, you outta start playing it, maybe with a little luck you might win! Hopefully it won't be too long to save up. I love seeing you on Tuesdays, but it's bittersweet… I feel sick to my stomach and heartbroken every time we have to hang the phone up. Every week I want to leave with you so bad my anxiety gets the best of me. It hurts watching you get up knowing you'll be driving so far by yourself in this shit weather, and I can't go with you. I really didn't mean for this letter to turn into an eight pager but, oh, well, more for you to read and it gives me something to do to help pass the time…lol. I figured I'd take a break from the puzzle books for a little while and write you a letter (well, a book) lol. I'm doing what I can to get these few weeks over quick as possible, so I broke my days into twelve-hour sections. I get meds about 6:30 A.M., breakfast @ 7:00 A.M., sleep till noon, get up call you, eat dinner @ 5:00 P.M., call you again, watch a little T.V. till 11:00 P.M., and repeat.

Right now, I've got twenty-seven days till court, which is also 672 long-ass hours. Yes, I just broke it down to the hour. :) I'm also glad you are in good hopes of me coming home on the third. I hope I do, too. So, I have four months of making up to do, huh? wink, wink!! Yeah, that should take our old asses all of fifteen minutes, then spend another half hour trying not to stroke out and catch our breath. LMAO!! But it'll be great either way. I really need a trim around the tree; it sorta looks like one of those treasure trolls with the wacky hair. I don't feel like myself at all, and I can't wait to start to feel remotely human again. I don't have a clue what fresh air is right now and freedom to walk around more than fourteen paces in either direction. I miss holding you at night and kissing you g-night. I feel so bare without you sleeping by me. Sometimes I still wake up with anxiety cause I was dreaming of us together again. I know these last few months have been hell for you, but I promise I'll make it up to you no matter what, and I'll do my best to keep you happy as possible. I can only hope it isn't much longer till we are back together. Of course, once again, all I have to offer is love since we have to start from scratch again. But I'm sure it won't be the last since we both want to go back down south. Okay, well, this will end up being a ten-pager…lol.

The guys in here keep asking me if I'm writing a biography. I tell them "no," I'm just chatting with the wife. They ask what all I could be possibly saying that takes nine pages. So, I say oh, just this and that. I love you, and I hope my letters don't bore you. I know it takes you a lot less time to read them then it does for me to write them. I'm curious, did you get my two blood pressure machines and my Green Bay piggy bank from TN? I'm sorry my letters are drawn out, but I really miss talking to you about any and everything. We used to sit either on the porch or in the bed and just talk, laugh and enjoy each other's company and being together. Now we've been apart for almost four, full months, and all we have is two, five- to ten-minute phone calls a night (which I'm very thankful for) and a fifteen-minute video visit in a crappy town and a shitty state that neither one of us should be in. They say what doesn't kill us makes us stronger, and I really believe that's true. But this is definitely testing that. I wish they would allow us to have pictures; it's stupid that they don't. They do a pretty good job at keeping us cut off as much as possible from society. Unless it's for court or visits, we never leave our cell. They have the phone cards so expensive, some people can't afford to call home, and commissary is just outrageous. I know it's a long shot asking you this cause I'm sure you probably don't know for sure yourself, but what do you suppose once I get out what our game plan will be? Any ideas? What would you like to do or see happen and in what kind of time frame? I'm so sorry you are involved in all this, but I'm glad you're by my side. I don't know what I would do without you. Right now, I'd have nobody to write, call, and no money. I hope this long-ass letter has kept you entertained at least for the whole five minutes it took you to read it...lol.

I guess I'll end this with I love & miss you very, very much and can't wait to be back together with you.

I love you more, most, mostest, always & forever, Amen!!!

Love Always Your Husband,
Jimmy


December 13, 2016

Hello, baby,

I love you and miss you so very much. I am sorry that I couldn't come see you for our weekly visit, but the weather was shitty and too cold to go anywhere. I feel like shit because I didn't come see you. Well, I go tomorrow to have my top teeth pulled, and I'm not looking forward to the pain I am going to be in. The dental assistant told me that I won't be able to have anything real hot for a few days, so no coffee for me in the morning and no sodas. So, there goes Mt. Dew, my liquid crack...lol

I will be on soft foods and liquid diet for a couple of weeks...yah me!!! Maybe I will lose a little of weight, but not too much. Ann and Tony have stuff here to make protein shakes, which the assistant said I needed to eat or drink things with a lot of protein and try to stay hydrated. This letter is going to be short because the card says everything that needs to be said.

I Love You,
Ri-Ri

December 16, 2016

Hey, honey,

I just got off the phone with you, and I'm glad you finally got in touch with Brown, but it doesn't sound like I'll be coming home on the third. I don't think he is doing anything to help me and even try to get me out. How can he not know what motions he's going to file when he's the one filing them? I'm really starting to believe he's also against me. Remember what I was saying in the beginning about the whole conspiracy thing? Well, it sure as hell seems like it. Why won't he even try to get me a bond reduction? Is he scared to ask? I'm thinking if something good doesn't happen and he doesn't even ask for a bond reduction then, we might need to start thinking about getting a new court appointed lawyer cause something is definitely going on. He seems aggravated every time I've talked to him. He can never seem to be able to tell me anything about anything, and it seems as if he just doesn't care. We really need to come up with money more than ever now. It seems that's all they want, and it's the only way I'm getting out of here. After I talked to you, I tried calling him and, of course, he was out of the office. Did you ask about getting me out on medical for my knee? Why isn't he doing anything? There are a couple of guys in here that have been here for seven months waiting for trial on drug charges.

I really need you to get us in the apartment ASAP, since he seems to think that's the only way I'll get a bond reduction. I don't see what the problem is with giving me a bond reduction. Don't they think I've lost enough with these allegations? And another thing that bothers me is every time I've seen or talked to Brown at court, all he really says is, well, the prosecutor isn't offering any pleas at this time. My question is why or how could he offer anything when I've done nothing to be guilty of. I'm not pleading to anything. In the end it'll be the judge that decides everything since Brown thinks it would be best if I had a trial by judge instead of jury. I just hope Brown isn't in on all of this and helping to keep me in here. It's hard to trust anyone right now, and it's as if the whole world is against me. Did he even mention or say how long it will take to get a trial? I don't think he's trying to help me. One of the charges carries a term of life for penetration. What's penetration, and where is the probable cause for that charge? In her testimony, she said I held a dildo up to her and said it wouldn't fit. I mean WTF? The judge said that was acceptable as probable cause. Surely Brown should already know to file a motion to have that dismissed. How is that even considered penetration? I'm no genius, but I have a feeling I'm getting the shit end of the deal and being left in here on purpose. Something has got to give, right?

How long does it really take to see this is all a bunch of lies? I'm not going to start rambling, but I just don't understand a lot of what's going on, and where the hell are our friends and family when I need them? I miss and love you so much, honey. Do you think we'll be in the apt. before court? I guess we need to get used to be apart cause it seems the situation isn't going to change. I just got off the phone with you, and it seems you have more trust and hope in Brown than I do. Besides that, even if I do get a bond reduction, I still wouldn't be able to get out cause you will pay the car payment and insurance, so we won't have any money and no one to loan us any. I'm just screwed and can't do anything about it but lay here. I'll probably be in here all the way till trial, which no one knows how long that will be, and then on top of everything else, they are trying to put me in prison for a crime I didn't do, and for some odd reason, it seems the whole town is in on it. It just puzzles me how and why they are letting multiple felony offenders go and I'm still sitting here. I can't even come up with fucking bond money. I'm at my last nerve on even trying to figure all of this out. I know one thing…I can't do anything to help my situation at all and my whole life is in Brown's hands, which isn't seeming to be a good thing since he isn't doing anything and showing no progress.

I do love and miss you very much. Some days go by better than others, and today is one of those days that existence is pointless. I guess it does pay to be a good guy, even in jail. One of the guys in here just bought me a calling card. He said it was because I helped him when he first got in here. I gave him a cup, a bowl, and shared my coffee & candy and drink mixes with him. So, at least now I can talk to you. Also, I've been trading my breakfast for coffee and a couple of the other guys share sometimes. Yeah, it's the pits not having money on my books, but I'd rather you hold onto it till court, so I might at least have a chance of coming home. I'm going to save as much of the calling card as possible, so I can call you on Xmas and hopefully New Year's. This is going to be a shitty way to start off 2017, but I can't do anything about it unless you hit the lotto. It might be a little bit before I write another letter cause I have to come up with some envelopes and stamps, but I'm sure I will figure something out. I wish I could just figure out a way to come up with bond money or a way for this nightmare to be over. I guess we will figure out what's going on in a couple of weeks. The way Brown is acting, I don't know what to expect. He seems so secretive and against telling us anything. Most lawyers try to keep their clients up to date and reassured on what may or may not happen. This guy seems not to give a shit either way how we feel or keeping us up to date.

Well its nine days to Xmas, eleven days till my b-day, sixteen days till New Year's Day, and eighteen days till judgment day. Does the four months I've been in jail even count towards anything? Have you asked him about that? I'd ask him, but I guess I don't matter cause I can't get ahold of him, and he damn sure isn't concerned on keeping me informed on anything or what wondering how I'm doing. I think the trustee is getting tired of sharpening my pencil...lol, he'll be okay. I feel like such an asshole for taking our time together for granted. I always said no one is promised tomorrow, but I never expected us to be kept apart like this. Neither one of us has any control as to what happens and when we will be back together, and it's not fair or right to either one of us. I'm sure I'm exaggerating and letting my mind get the best of me when I say some things, but I've never been in no serious shit other than my DUI, and I'm scared. I'm happy to hear Pete is still in contact with you and he is doing okay. I miss our old life. I want to go home. Well, I love you and good night, baby. I'll finish this letter tomorrow.

December 17, 2016

Hello, baby,

I'm glad I was able to get ahold of a calling card. I worry when I don't get to talk to you.

I guess I'll call just once a day, so I save time to call on Xmas and New Year's. I love and miss you, honey. I hope everything goes okay on the third. I keep hearing in here that Brown and Smith are good friends cause Smith was a popular lawyer here until he became the prosecutor and they used to work cases together. If any of this is true, then I'm fucked. Which I'm going to get screwed anyhow. Any other lawyer would have been fighting to get me out by now, don't you think? I'm tired of being in here under false pretenses and can't do anything to help or better my situation. I feel trapped. I was thinking about writing the judge a letter, but I don't know what Brown has planned. I'm going to be so pissed if Brown doesn't even try to get me out. I was asking people different things and had an idea. Why don't you write the judge and explain that since all of this has started I lost my job, we lost our apartment cause you couldn't afford it on disability, so we were forced to relocate here, we are currently staying with friends, but we are approved for housing, and we should be in it at any time. We both have Medicaid here, plus your disability is transferred here. Let him know we have nowhere else to go and I'm not a flight risk and you need me with you to get things back together, and I need to have my knee surgery. If the courts will allow it, maybe I can get house arrest or a tether and let him know all we have for money right now is your SSI. All we could possibly afford is a $500 and maybe $1,000 bond. I'm not sure if it'll do any good, but at least it would explain our financial and housing situation, just in case Brown doesn't come through for us. In your letter, also let him know as of January 3, I've been incarcerated for four months. Will you please write this letter to the judge for me? Or, hell, see if you can't talk to him personally, I know I'm asking a lot, and I'm not sure if you're comfortable in doing this for me, but I really need you and everybody is saying it helps sometimes if the spouse writes the judge. I'm sorry I ask a lot of you, but I'm not sure Brown will bring these things up in court to help get me out. I was thinking and I'm sure as far as the judge knows, I'm here alone and no residence or any chance of having a residence here and I still reside in TN. So, if he knows these facts when I go to court, then maybe I might have a chance. I just wish I knew more about the situation, I don't know nothing. All I know is they are tryin' to keep me in jail for a long time on something I didn't do, and I need to bond out to spend as much time with you as possible till trial, cause the way it seems, it doesn't matter if I'm innocent or if they have nothing to go on, either way I'm going to end up with something. I'm sure Smith and Brown are probably sitting around some where just deciding and contemplating on what they're going to do about this bullshit ass case. I'm sure they are just laughing their asses off and playing poker with my life. I bet if it was one of their family members, then they would've already have been home. Well, good night my sweet Maria. I love you and hope you have sweet dreams.


December 18, 2016

Hey, baby,

How are you doing today? It's been one of those long blah days. You know I've been sitting here rattling my brain for answers, and I got to thinking about the probable cause hearing, when Brown asked Rose how she knew what a dildo was, she said as she got older she figured it out. Well, Kathy bought her a video game one year for Xmas called Saints Row 3. Well, one of the main weapons is a huge, long, purple dildo called the penetrator. She said her mom and grandma was talking about me and it reminded her of things that happened. My question is, if I supposedly did show or touch her with a dildo, them why the hell didn't the game remind her? I'm sure Brown would get a kick out of that…well, maybe. Oh, don't think he's interested in anything I have to say. Well, sixteen days now. God, I hope I come home, but that will be difficult with no money. I've been in jail four months, and for what? Just so I'm not a flight risk. I'm starting to think I don't stand a chance in this corrupt town. I still have a feeling they know Kathy and they are on her side.

I guess I shouldn't get my hopes up in a town I don't belong in and don't know anyone. I wish I never stepped foot in this town. I just want to get on with my life (if I have one left). The closer it gets to court, the more my anxiety is getting worse. I've never ran from the law, missed a court date, or been violated on anything, so why won't the judge let me out till trial or at least give me a chance to post bond? Baby, you know me better than anyone, please either make an appointment to see him or write him a letter. Either way it probably won't help. We are outsiders, and Kathy is known by everyone one way or another. I'm sure she has pull here whether Brown says so or not. Why would he admit it to us anyhow? If he did then he knows it would be a conflict of interest then, and if he is in on some conspiracy, he wouldn't be able to help her. I feel so helpless, I wish I could afford a lawyer that no one around here knew than maybe I'd stand a chance. I don't know what to think anymore. I'm sorry you're mixed up in this shit. It's not fair to you that you're being bounced around and having to start over again. Ria, I'm scared. I know you are saying that Brown is doing what he can, but I'm not sure. I've done okay so far, keeping it together, but being locked in the same room twenty-four hours a day is taking its toll. I feel like a dog no one wants to adopt. I need fresh air and all this to be over. I can't hardly sleep anymore. I've been trading my breakfast so I don't have to wake up in the mornings. I do everything on my bunk; I eat, drink, sleep, do crosswords, and even now, I'm writing this letter while sitting on this fucking bunk. We never leave this cell. I'm out of envelopes and stamps, so this will probably be the last letter I'll be able to send till court. So, I hope you have a good Xmas and New Year's. I'll still call you on those days, though. I love and miss you so much. You know, I got so bored today, I got all my fruit I've been saving and put them in a bowl and put it on the table for a festive center piece, lol. The three guys in here got a kick out of it, and the guards said they loved what I did with the place…LMAO. Also, I just remembered in the probable cause hearing, she said that she asked me to let her get inside of my pants with me to see if she would fit, and I let her. The judge accepted that as a form of bodily contact, as to which the STD test was ordered. I mean, who the fuck would even believe that would even be possible? I don't wear baggy jeans for one, and two, that just sounds fucking retarded. There was a lot that didn't make sense, and I hope he tears her story apart like he said. But it's four months of my life I'll never get back, and they don't take that in consideration. I hope all this is just mandatory cause I'm sure a lot of times people are truly guilty, so they need time to sort shit out, but in my case, eight years is a long time, and I don't know why they even brought me back. That's why I think it's a set-up situation. I don't know who is out for me more, Rias or Kathy and Rose. I don't know, I guess I'll find out in a few days. I'm sorry this letter is so long, I'm probably just rambling, so I guess I will call while I can, see ya on visit if you can make it, and I will definitely see you at court. I hope you're able to bring money with you. We know I'm innocent, but how do we prove it? It all seems so unfair. I love you, baby. Goodbye for now, but hopefully not forever.

Love Always,
Jimmy
MERRY X-MAS and HAPPY NEW YEAR, BABY!!!!
XOXOXOX


December 29, 2016


Hey, baby,

I love and miss you so much. I wish Mr. Brown would have given me better news today, but we both knew that there was a probability that you wouldn't come home to me on Tuesday. I HATE IT, I HATE IT, I HATE IT!!!!! Since you have been in jail, my sense of security is gone, and I feel defenseless out here without you. I am lost and have nowhere to turn.

There is no sense for me to get that apartment now because I would be too scared to stay there by myself is she finds out where the apartment is. I asked Tony and Ann if it was okay with them if I stayed here with them, and they said that I could stay with them for as long as I needed to.

The craziness has begun here. Ann's brother, sister-in-law, and their three boys are here, along with Bonnie and Brad. So, there are eleven people in this house, but I still feel all alone. I am in my room, and they are all in the living room, but I'm okay with being by myself because that is their family and I really am not in the mood to be around people right now.

I'm sorry for telling you all of this, but I have no one else to talk to and don't want to burden them and put a damper on their family time. I put on a good face and try to act like everything is fine, but inside I am falling apart. I just don't understand why there is only one motion being filed, but maybe he has a strategy in mind and I hope the judge grants him the motion. Maybe he has an ace up his sleeve and just doesn't want to show his hand too early.

I love you baby and miss you so much. I miss sleeping next to you, holding you, and I especially miss your kisses. I just miss us, plain and simple!!!! That phone service that the jail uses is about to piss me off! Some days it works and other days, like tonight, it doesn't want to work at all, it's ridiculous!!! Friday is going to be even crazier because a friend of Tony's and his wife are coming and staying the night, so that will be thirteen people in the house. I am definitely hiding in my room. That is way too many people for me to be around.

I go back to the doctor next Friday to get a full check-up, blood work, and to talk to a counselor and see if I can't get something for my nerves. I'm also supposed to get my new glasses that day, too. Then on the eleventh, I go for my mammogram and then on the thirty-first, I go to Houghton for a consultation for a sleep apnea study.

Please, give me some advice on what to do about that apartment. I just don't know what to do and need your thoughts and opinion. I am trying my best to make this letter as long as possible, so you have something to read from me. I'm sorry this letter is depressing, and I don't mean to bring you down anymore.

I love you very much and don't ever doubt that. I am here for you, and I am doing everything I possibly can out here for you. I will never give up on you getting out and coming home. I am going to go for now, but not forever. I will write you again on Sunday when it is quiet and calm around here.

I LOVE and MISS YOU
Loving You Always & Forever, Amen,
Your Wife, Ria


January 3, 2017


Hey, baby,


It went how we thought it would. I'm probably going to be sitting here for another two months. We might as well forget bond all together and just ride it out cause we can't afford it. I'm not sure what all Brown said to you, but when me and him was alone before they brought me in the court room, he told me he didn't think the expert would be granted. I asked him if this motion is the only thing he is filing, and he said, no, no, there's a lot more he's going to do, but he doesn't want to let it out before trial cause he don't want to give Smith the chance to prep or coach Rose. So, to say everything before trial. In other words, he wants to catch her off guard. Also, he's talking about subpoenaing Det. Franks from TN since he conducted the initial interview. I really hope he can win this, but in the end, it will be up to the jury and the judge. When I left the courtroom, I seen Smith going towards his office, and I think Brown was in there too, but I could have sworn I heard them giggling to each other. Maybe I'm just paranoid. I don't know. I have been in here going on five months for two court sessions, and I feel like it isn't going anywhere. So, what's next? Another two months for Pre-Trial, then two months for trial? Has Brown even spoke with you about anything else? I really, really hope he proves to the jury this is all b/s. I don't know what to think; first, it seems he's not helping, then he seems to be trying to help me like today. I just got off the phone with you, and I guess including this month, I've got another four months till trial.

I guess it's better than waiting a year. I really hope Brown comes through for us. At least I got to give you a hug and a kiss today!! It's been so long, and I miss you so much. I do want you to do me a favor, though. I want you to ask Brown if something happens that we lose this case, what kind of time does he think I'll get since I've never been in serious trouble and never had a felony? I hope he can convince the jury I'm innocent. I know he says he believes he can but do or beat this against Smith, but it isn't left on Smith, it's the jury. That's what scares me. I'm tired of worrying, I constantly have a headache, and it isn't helping anything at all. Why is it even going this far? Is it so hard for Smith to see what's going on, so he puts it on other people to do his dirty work. I believe he doesn't know what to believe or think. I wonder if he knows all of this started over me not signing my rights away to my girls? Maybe that's one of Brown's wild cards. I also want you to ask him if he is at least going to try to have charges lessened or dismissed. Worst comes to worst, I can deal with fighting a five-year felony, but the one that carries life is what really worries me and ask him what the charges are now is what they will be then? I'm scared I'm going to never get out for a crime I didn't do. I always thought charges like murder or rape were life charges. I'm hoping he is going to get me out of this. Since the next step is pre-trial, both charges are probably what it'll be at trial. Why didn't he try to have the life charge dismissed or at least lessened?

I just don't really understand how the charge that carries life come about. Out of all shit why life? They make me feel so confused and helpless. Fuck, why not just go for the death penalty? At least it would all end, and I won't feel like a pawn in their chess game to be thrown away for life. OMG, just the thought of it makes me cringe. I'm definitely not going to be able to keep why I'm here a secret much longer. Also, the trial will be aired on Channel 8 news @ 5:00 or 6:00 P.M. We watch the news in here every day to see why new people are in here. They will be on there if its real serious, like meth raids and such. I wasn't and haven't been on there yet, but I'm sure the trial will be. That's what they were discussing today about the closed circuit T.V. The judge said they will use the poly-com. It will probably be on me the whole time and blocking out Rose. Also, Smith got it to where me and Rose won't have direct contact. One of the things Brown was hoping for was that she wouldn't be able to look me in the eyes and testify. He was hoping she would break down, but I guess that's out now. I wonder how many of these cases Brown has done and won? The same for Smith? I wonder if you could ask him or google him or something. How come all of Smith's motions and requests are being granted, but my stuff gets denied because I don't or can't afford to pay for a lawyer? How is that even fair? I should get the same opportunity to defend myself as everyone else.

I hope I'm getting treated fair. I'm curious as to what the judge thinks of all of this so far, and I'd like to know what was said or discussed in his chambers. They probably poured a brandy, cheered each other, and laughed at how they are putting on a good show for each other and talking on how they are sticking it to me, and I can't do nothing about it. I know you don't want me to think about it, but if all this goes to hell, what are your plans going to be? I'm sure you're not going to stay up here and believe me I have no intentions of going to prison. Please keep that to yourself, at least till afterwards. After the trial, if things don't work out, I'm sure I'll be sentenced right then, so I hope for the best. No matter what, please keep in touch and look after my father, please... He has no one else but Rosalie. I know I'm asking a lot for you to keep this conversation just between us, but you're my spouse and my best friend, so I hope I can trust you on this. I won't talk about it anymore, but I need you to promise on us and the grandkids, you won't say anything to anybody about my plans. If you agree and understand then write me back, just say, "Promise." I love and miss you so much, Ri-Ri, and I hope I've done enough to show you that. I know this letter went shitty, but I wanted to get all this out there, just in case. I guess I'm going to sleep. Good night, and I love you.

January 5, 2017

My dearest love,

I love you and miss you more than words can ever say! Well, Tuesday was a victory and a loss. The loss that we can't get an expert for your defense and a victory for the records. I am hoping Brown is able to pick apart the findings in those records and use them to his advantage to show this whole story is just that...a story that she made up in her head with a lot of help and coaching.

I will always believe in your innocence till the day I die!!! I have always believed in you and always will. Nothing and no one can or will ever change that. I wrote that song you wanted…that is a long ass song. It doesn't sound that long, but it is once you write it out...lol I found another song that you used to listen to all the time, "No Room in Hell," and if I find more, I will write them down for you. If you can think of any that you don't already have, just write them down as soon as you think of them and tell me on the phone or in your next letter and I will get them for you.

I will be coming to see you Tuesday no matter what the weather is like; two weeks not seeing you is too long. Well, I am going to finish writing that song for you and just remember…Don't ever give up because then she wins, and I'm not going to let that happen!!!!

I LOVE YOU, BABE
ALWAYS HAVE ALWAYS WILL
FOREVER, YOUR WIFE,
Ria


January 12, 2017

I love you and miss you baby. Here is a poem for you…

You Know, That You Know, When You Know
When you look into a person's eyes
Everything about that moment, sends shooting stars in the skies
When eyes are burning trough you
To where your soul can feel a touch
Your knees begin to buckle, and you can't stand without a crutch
You know, that you know, when you know!!!

Because when they're not around
You would do anything just to hear their sound
When we are together, life is so much more
You can't even remember what life was like before.

You know, that you know, when you know!!!

When your heart skips a couple of beats
Your palms begin to sweat
The feeling we get together
Is on we'll never forget!!!
Remember I love you forever and always, Amen


January 23, 2017

Hello, baby,

I love you and miss you very much. I loved your poem, and I am going to put a couple in this letter. I hope you get the pictures I drew, and I hope you like them. It is very important for me to express to you how much you really mean to me. I wish I could do this in person while holding you in my arms and gazing into your eyes. But since we are physically separated by miles of emptiness, this expression must come in the form of letters such as this. I know it is difficult for you, as it is for me, to be separated for so long. Life seems to be full of trials of this type which test our inner strength and, more importantly, our devotion and love for one another. Our love has been assaulted many times, and I am convinced that it is true because the longer I am away from you, the greater is my yearning to be with you again. I cherish any thought of you, prize and memory of you that rises from the depths of my mind, and live for the day when our physical separation will no longer be. Until that moment arrives, I send to you across the miles, my tender love, my warm embrace, and my most passionate kiss. If that wasn't enough...lol Here are some poems...

1.) Remembering
You were on my mind when I woke up this morning
remembering your smile
I guess the next time I'll see your face
might take a little while.

I was remembering your arms around me
the way they always felt warm
And having you right by my side
I completely felt no harm.

I was remembering your voice
it makes my heart skip a beat
but without you my love
my body feels so weak.

I was remembering our times
all the good and bad
the funny times you cheered me up
 and especially the sad.

I was remembering your eyes
how they always meet mine
remembering all the things you do
to make my life worthwhile.

I was wondering when we'll be together
when it will be just us two
I guess I'm just missing you
more than I usually do.

2.) Be With You
Each day I spent without you makes me
miss you so very much
Each night I dream about you

I long to feel your touch
If I could just see your face or kiss your gentle lips
If I could only hear your voice
All these little things I miss
So, I just want you to know
There's nothing I wouldn't do
If I could just once again Be With You.


3.) Forever and Always
Sitting alone under the stars so bright,
I wish you were here holding me tight.
Every day without you feels like eternity
I wish the day will come that you can be with me.
I miss your touch, your embrace, your smell
Why am I in this hole, my personal hell.
I miss you so much I can't help to cry
So much loneliness I'm about to die.
The memories we shared all seems but a dream,
But then I remember your sweetest word, that you love me
and need me,
I start to scream.
My love please come back I need your breath,
I will love you forever even after death.


4.) Have I Told You
Have I told you, you're handsome?
Have I told you, you're cute?
Have I told you I love you today?
Because if I haven't
I guess I forgot
It's something that I meant to say
You're handsome
You're cute
I love you, it's true
And I'm so lucky

To share life, with you!

5.) You're The Man
You're the man for me
In each and every way
You hold my heart caress my soul
Each breath I take for you
I would not want
Or need another
You're everything to me
And I will stay
Right by your side
For each and every day.

6.) How I Think of you
My brain is divided into three compartments,
the most secure area stores the memory of your face.
Above all things, I keep that safe,
a room with a sliding door
holds all the cute things you say.
Around my head,
they move freely through the day.
The last section is reserved
for all the things you love,
I keep those near and dear
This is how I think of you,
in the recesses of my mind.
This is how I think of you
100% of the time.

7.) I Miss You
Each morning I wake up
Thinking of you,
I remember you're not with me
And it makes me feel blue.

I miss your smile
I miss your touch
Sometimes my heart aches
I miss you so much.
I call you on the telephone
I write to you in a letter
You always tell me I'm not alone
You always make me feel better
I'm writing this to let you know
Just how much I love you so
Even though we're miles apart
You're right here beside me
Inside my heart.

Well, I think that's enough sappy shit for now...lol. I love you baby, and I will always love you. Your next letter will be more songs.

Loving You Always & Forever,
Your Wife, Ria


February 12, 2017

Hello, baby,

I love you and miss you especially on days like these. Today is definitely a bad day for me. All I feel like doing is cry. Ann was sick all day Saturday and then got up in the evening raising hell about everything, so I have stayed in my room, trying to stay out of her way. Then today they have barely said two words to me today, and I don't know what I have said or done for then not to talk to me today.

I am in a house with three other people, and I still feel all alone, almost to the point of feeling so out of place here and wishing you were here with me and telling me that everything will be alright. I try doing my cross-stitch to keep my mind busy, but that only lasts for so long, and then it goes back to thinking about how the hell she can be so devious and hateful to do all this shit to not just you, but us.

I don't mean for this letter to be so depressing for you, but I really don't have anyone to really talk to about my feelings. I am keeping everything bottled up because if I do talk about my feelings, I'm afraid I will totally break down and won't be able to pick myself back up again.

I have been taking my anxiety meds, but I really don't think it is working or it hasn't started working yet. Even though I have my trazadone, I don't get to sleep until about two-three in the morning and back up at seven-thirty or eight in the morning, so every day I am trying to function on about four hours of sleep every day, and sometimes I just don't feel like doing shit.

Ann tells me today, that her and Tony are going to quit smoking, so now I am going to have to figure out how to come up with money to buy my cigs, because with everything going on there is no way that I could quit right now. Smoking keeps my stress level down, so I don't flip out on people.

I just got off the phone with you, and I really couldn't tell you a lot with them in the next room. I'm just going to leave it alone for now and stay to myself. I'll just have to suck it up and deal with everything. I hope you like the cards I have gotten for you for V-Day. I know it's not the same as last year; hell, all of our special days have been fucked up, but that's okay, we will have plenty more days to celebrate together, and they will mean more than they did before because we both know how easily they can be taken away.

Today is just a bad day, and I am probably over-analyzing things and everything will be fine tomorrow. I can't expect every day to be just honky dory, I know there are going to be good and bad days, and I'm going to have to learn to deal with it. I love you baby and will write again.

Love always, Your Wife,
Ri-Ri


February 17, 2017

Hello, baby,

I know I have told you before how much I love you.
Here are 75 reasons what I love about you...

1.)  I love your beautiful blue eyes.
2.)  I love your cute smile.
3.)  I love your black hair.
4.)  I love your nose.
5.)  I love your body, everything about it.
6.)  I love how you never make me feel invisible.
7.)  I love how you breathe.
8.)  I love your sense of humor.
9.)  I love how you always make me smile even if I'm not in the mood.
10.) I love the way you look while you're asleep.
11.) I love how you make me feel wanted, complete and beautiful inside and out.
12.) I love the fact that when I dream of my future, I can only see you in it.
13.) I love how you still give me butterflies, even when someone mentions your name.
14.) I love how I can never imagine a life without you.
15.) I love how you understand me.
16.) I love how we're miles apart but I still feel safe and secure.
17.) I love how I can be myself with you.

18.) I love how you always think about me, even when you are asleep.

19.) I love how you can always know when something is wrong, even when I tell you I'm fine.

20.) I love you for trusting me.

21.) I love how you helped me through something that was hard.

22.) I love how you think my body is still beautiful, even though there are flaws on it.

23.) I love it when you call me "Baby Girl."

24.) I love how we have a song.

25.) I love how you think I'm cute when I cry.

26.) I love how you bring out the best in me.

27.) I love how you taught me to love myself.

28.) I love how you say I love you.

29.) I love the fact that we know we are getting married.

30.) I love how we talk about nonsense.

31.) I love how we saved each other.

32.) I love how I can look terrible and you still think I'm beautiful.

33.) I love the way you make everything okay.

34.) I love how we sometimes stay up and talk literally all night.

35.) I love your name.

36.) I love how we figure things out and work out the kinks in our relationship to make us stronger.

37.) I love how I'm halfway through this and it's so easy to write.

38.) I love the sound of your voice.

39.) I love your lips.

40.) I love how you make my head spin like a record.

41.) I love how you care about me.

42.) I love how you accept me.

43.) I love how we plan our future together.

44.) I love how I dream about you every night.

45.) I love how you think I look beautiful without any make-up.

46.) I love how you'll always be there for me.

47.) I love how I know I will always be there for you.

48.) I love how I need you.

49.) I love how good you treat me.

50.) I love how you respect me.

51.) I love how I'm comfortable with my body with you.

52.) I love how you hold the key to my heart.

53.) I love how you are my fiancée and my best friend at the same time.

54.) I love how you are my soulmate.

55.) I love how you are my strength and my weakness.

56.) I love how you make my heart skip a beat when you text me.

57.) I love how you're not like all the other guys.

58.) I love how you're soooo stubborn.

59.) I love how happy you make me.

60.) I love how I want to stay with you forever.

61.) I love how you never fail to amaze me.

62.) I love how I can look at a picture of you and smile.

63.) I love how you get a cute look on your face when you smile.

64.) I love how I can vent to you.

65.) I love how I think of you 24 hours a day.

66.) I love how we can be silly with each other.

67.) I love how you take my breath away.

68.) I love how serious we are about each other.

69.) I love you for you.

70.) I love how much we mean to each other.

71.) I love how you trust me even though you've been hurt by other women.

72.) I love how you hug me from behind.

73.) I love how you kiss me on my forehead for no reason at all.

74.) I love how you call me "Pretty" and we both know what that means.

75.) Babe, I love you; and no one can ever change how I feel about you.

You're going to be the one I marry and live happily ever after with. I pinky promise. I love you and I hope by now you know I truly mean it from the bottom of my heart.

Well, it is about 11:30 P.M., and I am going to try to get some sleep. I love you and will send you the songs in my next letter.

I LOVE YOU ALWAYS & FOREVER!!
Your wife, Ria


February 10, 2017

Hello, baby,

I got your Valentine card with your seventy-five reasons in it and that made me smile and reminded me why I love you so much. I miss everything about you, and I'm very grateful to have you in my life as my love and my best friend! I'm sorry I can't be with you this Valentine's Day, but we will be back together soon. Tell the girls (.)(.) and the whooha :) I love and miss them so very much...lol!!! I know you're tired of the snow, and I'll be glad to get back to our fishing trips also. I'm glad you finally got ahold of Brown. Why is the trial going to take four days and I'm hoping I can keep it all together until this is over. I still haven't heard anything about getting moved to a two-man cell, so I guess I'll have to ask again. I'm hoping I can, so it would be less to deal with. Also, what's the point of the pre-trial if nothing changes and he doesn't plan on filing any more motions? Although I feel he should be filing a motion and at least should be fighting to try and get the charges lessened just in case, but he isn't.

I might be able to keep the first hearing hidden but once it all starts in April, it's going to be impossible then. If you can, will you please email Brown and ask him to please not send me a letter for the pre-trial? I know when court is. Every time I get law mail, people get nosey and wanna know what it is or what it's for. Under the circumstances I would appreciate it. That way when I get back in here March 7, I can just say I had to meet with my lawyer and the D.A. and he had it continued till April. That would get me at least through March. I hate having to lie so much, but I know for a fact no one would understand or give me a chance to explain, so then it becomes a safety issue. So, if you can explain to him to not send a letter over, then it would help me a lot! If it's mandatory, then see if he could just send them to you. I know I've said it a million times, but I hope I've done enough to tell you or let you know how much I love you. Thank you for telling him I didn't mean to offend him, I'm just going a bit loopy in here. I feel good about him, although I have no choice but it really helps that you firmly believe in him and he'll get me home. Ask him if he has to send me something like that, so I don't have to explain much. I love and miss you, honey. I just hope these next few months go by quick and I come home to you in April.

Since he told you not much is going to happen March 7, I guess I don't have much to look forward to until April, unless he pulls a rabbit out of his ass we don't know about. Today looks like it might be a decent day. Well, the sun is shining through our so-called window, so maybe it'll warm up soon. Being here, this place makes me feel like an anomaly in this world, like I don't matter or exist. That's why I'm glad I have you to help me stay strong during all this. I would have no one and nothing to look forward to. As you can see even my own family is blowing me off. I love and respect Tony and Ann for everything they have done for us. Well, mainly for you. One thing that is bothering me though is that Brown suggests I don't testify. Doesn't that make me look bad or guilty? Will the jury hold that against me or look down on me for that? Also, how can I defend myself against anything said that he hasn't been made aware of or doesn't know how to answer? Like Smith thought, I flipped out when all of this started because of guilt, but if he knew anything about me, he'd know I did the same when my mother and Theresa passed away. I don't handle tragic events or stress too well. It don't have shit to do with guilt; it's a mental disorder, I believe. Besides, all they would have to do is pull my medical records. They are just going by what they think instead of going by facts. Is he going to use the statements or all the research you've done on the light bulbs? Or any of the other info we gave him?

I'm lost and confused as why he won't use Tony and what I'm supposed to do to defend myself without character witnesses or anybody on my side. It doesn't seem fair that she will have the town and family with and for her, and I have no one. I know he said he doesn't like to lose, but it kinda feels from my view of things that I'm being set-up for failure, but they don't want to make it obvious, so I don't know what to do, say, or think. All I can do is put my trust and faith in God and Brown to get me home and through this. But like I said so many times, there's nothing we can do but wait and see. It shouldn't take four days for people to see this is b/s. Kathy stated in the report that something happened to me in Indiana, but she didn't know what cause I never talked about it. You might want to let Brown know that I lost my kids for being unfit. I couldn't keep a place or job, so he'll know if it is brought up. I don't know if Smith will look into it or not, or if it's even relevant, but at least he will know. I'm really trying to help him here, so he has no surprises.

Let him know no one was charged for anything; we just couldn't get our stuff together. This happened I believe in 2002-2003. They say everyone has a purpose. I wish I knew what mine is. Thank you for loving me, even though I'm a basket case. I do hope I come home to you soon. I'm sorry I can't be with you for Valentine's Day, but believe this...I'm thinking of you 100 percent. I love and miss you deeply and just remember we have got to hope that we'll be reunited soon.

As far as clothes for court, I'm not sure I have anything court-worthy, and my shoes have the laces out of them, and my belt is here in my property bin up front. I don't know if I've got any jeans that aren't stained. I'm so beside myself, I've never felt so helpless in my life. Like everything I do is a lost cause. The good news is this month is halfway over. Twenty-five days till the pre-trial, three weeks and four days. It's getting closer, but not close enough. Then another four weeks for Doomsday to be over. I love and miss you so much, baby girl. I don't know what to think or do, but as time goes slowly by, I just hope and pray that this all ends soon, and we can get outta here and back to livin' our life together. I will write a longer one as soon as I get more paper...

I love you and I hope you have a good Valentine's Day!!!

I'm always thinking of you, babe!

I love you always & forever,
Jimmy
HAPPY VALENTINE'S DAY, BABY GIRL!!!


February 22, 2017

Hello, Ri-Ri,

I'm not sure what's going on, but I hope you are okay.

When I talked to you last, you said you would come see me, but I guess you didn't have gas money since you didn't show up. It sucks not being able to talk to you to know what's going on or if you're okay. I'm worried sick. I got a letter from Brown yesterday, just telling me about court, and it says this will be the final time and chance for Smith to offer any deals. I also haven't had any mail. I guess you don't have stamps. I hope you get your check soon. It's messin' me up bad not having any contact at all with you. Now I really feel alone in the dark. It's the whole not knowing. I don't know anything. I hope we don't go this long without some sort of contact ever again. I want so bad to hear your voice, just to know you're okay. Last night, when you didn't show up, my heart sunk, and I just laid, staring at the wall until I finally went to sleep. I know it's my mind getting the best of me, but I hope you didn't give up on me, too, and that you just haven't had money for gas. I know you wouldn't do that, but in here all thoughts are possible. I miss you so much. I miss your voice, smile, and everything else about you.

This whole situation is a damn disaster. I feel like the only way it's going to end or get any better is if I just don't wake up, but I'm still here. I don't deserve any of this, and it's tearing me apart. I just want it to be done and over with. God, I hope nothing's wrong and you are okay. Hopefully, I'll get a calling card soon, so I can call you, so I'll know it was all in my head and you're okay and are still here for me. I'm also hoping I get to see you next Tuesday. This is destroying me little by little. There are so many thoughts in my head, and all I can do is sit here and stare at the wall and keep thinking. I have no one to talk to about how I feel or the things that bother me, and it's taking its toll. Even more now since I can't talk to you, either. Donnie let me use his card, so I could call you. I'm glad nothing's wrong and you are okay. I figured you still haven't gotten money yet. It's so reassuring to hear your voice; it's hard to keep from thinking of stupid shit in here. I love and miss you, honey.

Tell Andrew and Shay I'm sorry they are going through all of that shit. I feel like in a way it's my fault they're in that position. Did he get a car yet? What did Johnny say about it all? Tell him I love him and keep his head up. I'll help figure things out as soon as I can. Does he still have his job? So, court is March 7 @ 10:30 A.M. I'm tired of being in here and want to get on with life while I still have one. It says in the paperwork Brown sent me that this hearing will be the last for Smith to offer a plea deal. Ya know, he won't, but if he did, I'm almost tempted just to get it over with. There has got to be an end. I'm tired of worrying about everything. I'm sending the paper work, but apparently Smith has to provide a list of witnesses and an exhibit list that are going to be used to Brown by Friday, March 3. So, you need to call him Friday to find out what it looks like. If I don't get or accept a plea deal on the seventh, then Brown will have to provide the same by Friday, March 10. Find out from Brown if he thinks Smith will offer anything and does he think if it would be worth one to take it? I'm scared and want to come home.

If Brown has to have everything together by the tenth. Why haven't you or Tony been subpoenaed yet? Is he not going to use ya'll? WTF? So, what the hell is he going to do or use to defend me? I'm scared. How can he defend me with nothing to work with? He will know everything Smith is working with against me by Friday the third. I'm very thankful for my coworkers to write out the statement, if they can. What really bothers me is when Brown said, "As long as we can get at least one person on the jury to say not guilty, then we could appeal it." Why would he say that? Does he think I'll lose? There is no physical evidence; all there is testimony. I don't get. I feel like I'm being set-up. I don't know, honey, something just don't seem right. I hope whatever is in her counseling records is enough to help me. I don't see how they can charge me with the things they are without anything. That's what has me boggled. I just wish I knew what the hell is really going on. I'm stressed the hell out. Hopefully Brown can sort out and know how this is going to go on the seventh and then the trial.

I know he's busy with other cases and such, but he's had limited contact about anything. I'm lost and confused, and don't know what to think. I hope he uses all of the statements that you get along with your research. From what I've seen, everyone that has gone to trial here is getting fucked. Another cellmate just went through trial was found guilty on seven felonies and got sentenced to thirteen years. The D.A. offered him four years before trial, and he turned it down and took it to trial. Why is my trial going to take four days? I don't understand or deserve any of this. Just please get with Brown to find out what I'm against and figure shit out. I'm going to end this letter, so I can send you court papers with it. Thank you for everything you are doing, and I love and miss you so much.

Love You Always,
Jimmy

February 25, 2017

Hello, my love,

I love you and miss you so much. Where to begin? I am writing to you to remind you of how much I love you. I would first like to start off by telling you that never in my life had I thought that I would ever find someone who loves me the way you do. You are my one and only; my past, present, and future, and my soulmate. This is something my niece shared on FB, and I thought I would share it with you...

Life is Scary

One day you wake up feeling like you can take over the world, and the next day you wake up feeling like all you want to do is lay in bed and hide from everything. People walk into your life, grab your hand, and lead you into the most beautiful path you've known, yet sometimes the same people let go of your hand with no warning, and you become stranded at a place where you never thought you would feel lost.

Let's be honest, sometimes everything is going so great, and it seems like nothing could go wrong; but right when you begin to think that, something so horrible comes crashing down, and all of a sudden, more problems come ricocheting around you, and you just feel so hopeless because it feels so bad…so frickin' shitty!

It's hard to understand why such things happen in life, and I personally wish I had an answer to that "why" you always ask yourself, but all I can say is no matter how hard life gets, you have to keep going.

The life around you will never stop going on. I'll be honest and say that sometimes makes me feel a bit worried, and it gives me anxiety because all I can think is, "Will I be able to keep up? What if everything goes too fast?" But I realized that being scared and living with that burden of running away from problems only slows me down even more. And I've come to the point where I believe that because life never stops, I shouldn't stop, either. It's okay to take breaks and to give yourself time to heal, but you cannot give up and you cannot quit.

There is so much waiting for us to do and we simply can't give fear the satisfaction of winning when we can give success, growth, and accomplishment that same satisfaction, if not even more. Please believe in yourself and encourage yourself instead of doubting yourself. Keep it positive, fill your heart with gratitude for what you already have, and always remain humble and true to who you are. Because even if life is hella scary, not living it is scarier!!!

I read this and thought about what has happened to us since May 2016 when all of this bullshit started and thought how much our lives have changed. We cannot give up on anything or quit trying to get you home where you belong. I love you, baby, and will write again soon, but I have to write your songs.

Loving You Always & Forever,
Your Wife, Ria


March 10, 2017

Hello, beautiful,

Today Mr. Brown's secretary came to see me to sign a paper to get the counseling records. She also left me a packet with a copy of the request and a copy of the Facebook message with Kathy saying my signature isn't going to be needed. He also included some info on a genetic disease called E.D.S.-Ehlers-Danlos Syndrome that Kathy claims in the Facebook message that Hailey has. I remember that discussion, and Kathy says the test was negative. But Brown seems to think since it's genetic that Rose would have it, too. I'm sending you the copy of the request. I know for a fact Rose was born severely premature and with cerebral palsy, pfft, even the FB message shows how pissy and vindictive she can be. I'm almost to the point where I just don't care anymore and say fuck it, go to trial! I'm tired of being scared and worrying, so let's get it over. If I lose, at least I go down swinging. I have a lot of faith in my lawyer. If it goes the way it should, I'll be free of all this in a few weeks. I'm not going to lie, I'm scared but I won't go down without a fight. If I lose, I go to prison, and I'll be on the registry. If I plead out, yea I'll be out of jail soon, but I'd be on the registry, owe fines and fees, plus I'd be reliable for the transportation here. If I go to trial and win, I go home, owe nothing, and can put this state behind me. But I still have a lot of if's and insecurities. I'm pretty sure that penetration charge isn't going to hold up, so that leaves the second which is a fifteen-year felony. I don't know what to think about it, but I guess we'll know Tuesday, and I'll make a decision then. I love and miss you.

So, option A, wait till Tuesday, find out what Brown has to say. and take a plea, or option B, go to trial and take a chance. I think the only way I'll take a plea is no prison or registry. Otherwise, let's get this show over with, so I can get it done and go home. I'm tired of entertaining this county. I along with a lot of people know without a doubt I'm innocent, now we just have to get that through to a jury. That's the part that scares me. I'm going to keep this letter short, so I can include some of the papers Brown sent to me. I love and miss you.

How do you think it's going to go if we go to trial now that you had that meeting with him? I'm sure he told you more than he's told me. I'm sure there's a lot he can't say to me as far as suggestions. I guess I have to decide some things for myself. This is the biggest decision I'll ever have to make. It's human nature to preserve one's existence and freedom, which is steering me toward a plea. I'm truly scared and worried about the outcome of trial, but I know it's the right thing to do to prove my innocence, and move on. I guess what it comes down to is knowing and proving I didn't do this. I'm not comfortable taking a fall for something I didn't do, but I guess Tuesday will decide it all, so I can come to a final decision on the rest of my life. I love you and will write again soon! Oh, I can't wait to see you again Tuesday. Make sure you read the papers good and tell me what you think. Exhibit A...is the Facebook message you printed off and gave to him. Exhibit B & C....are just info on the disease. Make sure Brown knows Rose was a preemie and has cerebral palsy, and has had surgery to correct her foot.

Love You Always,
Jimmy

March 16, 2017

Hello, my husband,

I love you and miss you very much. I hate that you are back in that place that took me so long to get you out of. I need you to stay positive and defiant!! Because I know you're innocent, Mr. Brown knows you're innocent and you know you're innocent, and now we have to prove to the jury with that same defiance and attitude that you're innocent. All hope is not gone! I have probably written this to you before, but I thought after today I feel like I need you to read it again.

"I Love You"

"I love you" means that I accept you for the person that you are, and that I do not wish to change you into someone else. It means that I will love you and stand by you even through the worst of times. It means loving you even when you're in a bad mood, or too tired to do things I want to do. It means loving you when you're down, not just when you're fun to be with.

"I love you" means that I know your deepest secrets and do not judge you for them, asking in return that you do not judge me for mine. "I love you" means that I care enough to fight for what we have and that I love you enough not to let go. "I love you" means thinking of you, dreaming of you, wanting and needing you constantly, and hoping you feel the same about me. I Love You!!

I don't want you to lose faith or hope. The truth will come out and we will prevail. We are in this together, what happens to you happens to me. When you're scared, I'm scared. When you're down, I'm down. When you're confused, I'm confused. When you're defiant, I am defiant. When you're confident, I'm confident.

Do you see the pattern here? We have to be strong, confident, and defiant together!! You are my whole world, and I need you to stay strong and hold your head up high and let them see that they aren't getting the best of you or that they are wearing you down. I know it's hard to do, but that is what they want you to do is break. STAND YOUR GROUND!!!! BE DEFIANT!!!!!

I love you very much and I know that stubborn side of you, now all you have to do is: BRING IT THE OLD JIMMY and show them that you are innocent and STAY TRUE TO YOURSELF!!!
Loving You Always & Forever,
Amen

I am and always will be your loving wife,
Ri-Ri


April 6, 2017

My beautiful, Maria,

I love and miss you so much. I guess things went to shit. I think you should maybe go stay with Andrew & Shay. I'm sure they could use your help. I really don't want you here by yourself and with the car payments and insurance, I don't know how you will survive alone. I've got six months in now, so when sentencing comes around, I'll probably have eight ten months in. I have no prior felonies, and my guidelines are low, so maybe he will give me time served with a few years' probation. One of the guys in my cell said when he got his first felony, he had two, one-to-ten-year and 1 four-year, and he got county time. I talked to Brown and sentencing is May 16, and he suspects I'll get three years. I have no trust and faith for the system at all. I'm not sure what will happen or where I will go, but I'll do my best to get through it, so I can get back to you. If you don't wait on me to get out or you want to move on, I'll understand. You deserve a good life and so much more than I have or could give you.

This system and county knew everything that was going to happen or what to do with me. I still believe in my very first thought, "conspiracy." There was so much more that could've been done and used to prove me not guilty, but he didn't. I think he and Smith came to an agreement while we were in the law library, waiting on the verdict he asked me again if I wanted to accept the plea. I guess I should have since I got stuck with the same anyhow. I'm worried about you. Neither one of us deserve this. They had no evidence to go on to say I did anything, but it's too late and done now.

My life is never going to be the same. I'm done with hope, praying, trusting, and thinking things might turn around. There is no justice these days. I do not believe in the system and never did. They had me convicted when I walked in the room. I thought if I didn't testify, it would hurt me, but in reality, it didn't matter what I did or said. This whole thing was put together from the get go. I'm not sure if Brown sold me out or not, and it seems like the judge was all for Smith from the get go. This whole community stands behind their own, and I was an outsider that they didn't give a damn about. But three years is better than a minimum of twenty-five years.

It will be awhile, but we will be back together. Life is short as it is, but ours just got shorter. Do you think we will ever be happy again? My worst fear is that something would happen to you and my dad. What would I do then? I would be all alone with no one. The only two things I can look forward to now is getting through this as best and quick as possible or to die in my sleep peacefully. I'm not a quitter, and I will get through this. I'm missing you so much; I didn't want to let go of you at all yesterday, but I didn't want you anymore upset than you already were. The day you come to my sentencing, I'll need you to come to the jail and pick up all my belongings. All my hygiene, clothes, our letters and anything else I have here. I'm not allowed to take anything with me except 1 piece of paper with addresses and phone numbers. I'm scared, and I hope I survive this, but I'm going to try.

I know when I leave here it will be about thirty days for me to go through intake and get situated where ever they put me. So, unfortunately, we will have no contact for about a month. I love you so much and just want to be at home in your arms. There are a couple of songs I want you to listen to. If you want to send me the lyrics you can, but I would like a couple of letters from you letting me know how you are feeling and what your plans are. God, I'm so sorry you're feeling all alone and we aren't together. Baby, what are we going to do? I mean, how are we going to get through this? From what I hear, people with CSC charges are generally kept housed together and are pretty much secluded from everyone else, but I'm not sure.

I'll tell ya, I still say I didn't get treated fairly. She got exactly what she wanted, and she knew she would. That is what I call a make-believe trial. The only thing that says I did anything was Rose's testimony. There wasn't even a proper investigation. I wish I knew someone or an organization to help me fight this. What about the Innocents Project? Do some research and see if there is anyone or anything we can do besides my appeal. I don't see how they can do this to me and get away with it. Please don't stop trying to fight this for me; you are all I've got to look forward to when I do finally get out. Just remember, no matter where I'm at or how long it becomes, I love you and we will be together again. Our love will go on it's going to be hard to get through it, but I'll try if you do.

I feel like I am crashing head first into a wall, and I need you and a miracle right now more than ever. Once you find out where I'll be, please write me as much as possible. At least there I can have pictures and cards. They even sell radios and headphones, T.V.s, and shavers and things. I guess you get assigned a job there and you get $0.40 an hour, which is paid monthly, and they even take taxes out. Isn't that fuckin' nuts? With working and all, maybe it will go by quick. Brown said he will be with me for sentencing to make sure Smith doesn't railroad me. He said he might be able to argue a few points to get a lesser sentence. I don't know if I believe him. With no proof and guideline sentencing, he says three or four years, but I don't know what Smith will do because he can put in a recommendation.

It's a fifteen-year felony, so I know it won't be more than that. This is and will be the biggest challenge of our lives. If we get through this together, then we will have the rest of our time on earth together. I keep asking myself, why is this happening to us and why is God punishing me? There is no reason I should be here. This county and the people in charge of the laws here are corrupt. This would never be going on in TN. Maybe the next life will be better for us, maybe things would have been different if I would've had a paid or better lawyer. I don't think Brown gave it his all or he had worked it out with Smith when they were in the judges' chambers.

After the verdict came back, and it was all said and done, he and Smith seemed to be all buddy, buddy and shaking hands and laughing. I didn't find it funny at all. I got an unfair, bum trial. I thought I had a right to even a mistrial. I want to come home, and now I can't for years. My whole world is out of whack. The judge could keep me in county if he really wanted to, but I'm not holding my breath. I'd have no problem doing a whole other year here. I'm scared to go to prison.

Either way, I want you to take care of yourself and do what you need to in order to be safe, secure, and happy. Please keep in touch with me as much as possible; you are all

I got left. This county had it out for me since I got here. I watch the show Another 48 and people are getting four years left and right for man slaughter and murder. It seems wrong for the judge to throw the book at me on my first felony. There are people here with multiple twenty-year felonies and getting a county time, but Brown is dead set on me getting two-four years in prison. I think it's all a conspiracy, and it was planned to go this way. That's why Brown was so adamant on me to take the plea deal. He knew it would go like this anyway. Doesn't anyone else think something is wrong with this case? You should go online and find out how much a good appeal lawyer is. How do I know for sure no one on the jury panel knew Kathy or someone in her family?

I know something was wrong with this trial; the jury didn't waste any time on a verdict. My life was taken within a couple of hours with no evidence. I want out of the north...period. I guess save as much as possible, so when I do get out you can rent a place, so I'll have somewhere to parole to. I'd prefer to be in TN, please, if you don't mind. I hope my dad is okay and holds out until we get back. Well, if I get back. Any suggestions on how I can get through all this without giving up? They made me feel and look like a worthless piece of shit. I have nothing left to give, so now they want to take my life to. I'm being treated like a murderer. I don't know how I'm going to get through all of this. In a place like prison, anything can happen, and we aren't promised tomorrow.

I wish I could change all of this and give you the life you deserve but, once again, I have failed you. I'm so sorry, I feel like I've abandoned you when you need me the most and I can't do or change nothing to keep you close, safe, secure and happy in this life with me. I don't know why you waste your time with me, I wish we could go back to the first day we met and start over. I guess I was stupid to not see that we belong together and now we are apart once again.

You and my dad are all I have, so please keep him as well as yourself safe and healthy and please don't give up on me. I love and miss you dearly and hope you know that. I'll write and call as much as I'm able to. I guess I'll quit rambling on and say I love you and bye for now, but not forever. Pray for me.

Love Always & Forever, Amen
Jimmy


April 7, 2017

Hello, my love,

I love you and miss you so much! Wednesday, after the verdict and the guards let me see you (thank them for that from me), I didn't want to let you go or leave you because I was afraid that was going to be the last time that I get to hug you or kiss you for a long time. I am still in shock and disbelief of the verdict. How the jury didn't see through the lies that Kathy and Rose told, the shoddy investigation that wasn't done, the lack of any evidence and all of the inconsistencies, how they found you guilty of anything is beyond me.

There was so much more that could have been brought out in this trial that wasn't. I have a good mind to write the judge and the editor of the newspaper and voice my opinion and let the people of that county know the things that were not told in this trial. Tell them who the real monster is and how you were the victim as well, in that relationship. She doesn't walk away from this squeaky clean, like she did nothing wrong.

I will need your help to decide whether to stay here in Michigan or go back down south. I don't want to leave you here in this god forsaken state while you're in prison, but I will have nowhere to live after June 1. I just wish they would give you five-ten years' probation and let you transfer everything to Tennessee and we can both go back south together.

I just got off the phone with your dad, and he told me to tell you that he loves you and that I needed to come back there and that I wouldn't have to worry about a place to stay because they will help me. I have had offers from Jessica, Cindy Bertch, and your dad to come stay with them, but I want your opinion where you think I should go or where you think I would be better off at. I know that is a lot to ask of you, but this is a decision that I would like to make together, just like we do everything else.

I know this is a lot to ask of you with everything that is on your mind and with the sentencing date set for May, and I don't want to put more pressure on you with my problems that I have out here. Thursday was not the day that I needed to be bombarded with what I planned on doing or with the bullshit from your sister. I was still an emotional wreck and still trying to process the verdict from the night before. I wasn't able to gather my thoughts or have time to myself to process anything.

I don't want you to ever worry about me ever leaving you because that is never going to happen. I will be here. now and forever. I will be waiting for you outside those walls where ever that might be, standing there with arms wide open and ready to bring you home where you belong with me. You are stuck with me forever!!! LOL

When you get where they are going to send you, I will send you pictures, letters, and all the songs that I have written you, so you will have things to read. Maybe they will allow you to have care packages of things like books, snacks, or any other things you need or would like to have. I will send you that stuff.

I just wish we could get married before you get sentenced and sent off because without being married some prisons won't release information about an inmate unless you are a spouse or a close relative. I checked on it, so ask one of the guards if it is possible that we can get married, so I am not completely in the dark about where you end up going and I am down as your wife and legal emergency contact. I know this right now this the least of your worries, but it is something that needs to be considered and done.

Well, I just got the mail, and I guess my decision has been made for me about where I am going to live. I got a letter from housing and it says that the current basic rent plus utilities exceeds 45 percent of my adjusted monthly income that my application for housing here in Michigan will not be considered for an apartment. So, I called housing in Harriman, TN, and she told me that if I can pay the $624 that I owe them, that I could get into a place, even if it is Clifty Manor. So, I guess I will be going back to Tennessee to live and take care of our dad.

I called Brown's office, and his assistant told me that a Justice of the Peace or the magistrate would be able to marry us. So, I am going to call on Monday and find out when and how much it will be to get a marriage license and find out when this can be done. I know this isn't how either of us wanted to get married, but we can do it the right way when you do come home.

I love you, baby, and you are and always will be my whole world. I know that I am going to have to learn to adjust to life without you there and do things on my own, but it won't be forever. We will be back together again and never be apart again!!!! I will write you again soon, and I will be there Tuesday to see you. I love you and miss you, and I will see you soon.

Loving You Always & Forever,
Amen
Your wife forever, Ri-Ri

April 15, 2016

Hello, beautiful,

How are you hanging in there? I'm best to be expected, I guess. Tomorrow is Easter, and I miss you so much. I don't mean for this to sound wrong, but I'll be glad when you're safe back in TN. I worry about you and my dad, and I know you will be safe and happier there. With a little hope, I'll be back there with you. I've got exactly four weeks from tomorrow till court again. I'm praying for the best and a quick appeal. That's about all I got left. I know after May 16, they can do no more to me; it'll finally be over. The next step from there would be an appeal. I'm trying to stay positive, but in this county, there's no such thing. I'm just to the point now where I'm over it, and I just wanna do whatever it is to come home. Good thing I guess is I'll have seven months in at sentencing. I keep telling myself although it may seem like it, it can't last forever. I love and miss you. Because of all this, I don't know how we will or can get life back on track. If I don't get this over turned life will never be the same. It sucks we can't find anyone to help me. If we were rich, I wouldn't be here and acquitted on both charges. I feel I'm being singled out and being punished for having no money. Where's the fairness and justice in that? Isn't there anyone pro-bono that isn't in it for the money? Well, I guess you get what you pay for, and I guess that's why Brown left me hanging with whatever he and Smith came up with. I've sat here long enough to know this county is corrupt and unjust. I miss TN so bad.

I just hope and pray they get done tormenting and torturing me soon, so I can just get on with what life I have left. By having this one charge, my life will never be the same, and they have taken so much from me I'll never get back or be the same. If this gets appealed I'll never be in this situation ever again. The appeal is the only hope for saving what we have left. With me carrying this charge, why would you even still want to be with me, let alone marry me? Don't you know it will affect you, too? You're pure as a woman can get and you should stay that way. I don't want you labeled, too; that isn't fair to you. I guess I've only got one chance at an appeal. How many times can I appeal it? Can't I take this all the way to Supreme Court? I'm not sure how any of this works. Well, I'm going to get some sleep. Tomorrow is Easter, so I'll be good and depressed and write more. I love you.


April 16, 2017

Happy Easter, Ria,

Well, another holiday gone. I hope you have a good day. Today is just another day for me. It's not the same, so I just skip it. There's been a lot of those days. This fucking county and Kathy managed to pull off what they set out to do, so why won't they just let me go home to try to salvage what little bit of a normal life I've got left? Today is just a shitty day. I'm tired of just laying here wondering what's going to happen. Al least we'll know in about four weeks. I wonder if Brown is going to try and at least ask to keep me in county or at least ask for minimum sentencing. No matter how it all goes, I know I've never got to see these people or this county ever again. Still, four weeks seems like forever, and then only God knows what I'm facing. I'm just ready to get on with it, so I can come home, if I have one I'm able to go to. I'm afraid I won't be able to get a job or find a place to live. What do I do then? Do I just exist as a bum in a ditch with no chance of a decent life? I'm scared. The judge can give me whatever he wants. I just hope he sees I got a bad verdict and gives me the minimum. He could overturn it, but Brown already said my chances of that was below zero. Besides that, you know Smith is going after the max, and I don't know yet what the probation/parole officer is going to recommend, but as soon as I see her, I'll let you know. The good thing is the judge doesn't have to go by anyone's recommendations. I'll see the probation officer a day or two before court. Brown has already told me to suck up and kiss her ass as much as possible, in case the judge follows her recommendation. I don't see how anyone up here has hope or trust or fairness in the court system. No wonder the jail is so crowded all the time, and from what I've heard, the Michigan prisons are even worse crowded. The people here don't like me that's obvious, so don't expect us to be able to get married till I'm free again. From the looks of things and from what all I've heard, that could be a while if he chooses. I love and miss you so much.

I don't know really what to think since trial. I should've known the way Brown kept trying to get me to plea, how it was going to go. I also know he wasn't in it 100 percent to get me freed. Isn't there anyone else you can call to get me help or anything else we could do? I don't deserve this; I'm wanting my old life back. We were happy and doing okay. I guess the loan I got last year is on my credit by now, which sucks cause with the car and that loan it would've built my credit back up. Hell, with this charge, I'm not going to need credit and should just file bankruptcy. I have nothing anyway, and probably never will have again. Please, whatever happens or whatever you do, please don't give up or lose the car; it's the only decent thing we have left. I'm sorry you got stuck paying the car payments and insurance by yourself. Believe me, I'd rather be working and helping you with the bills. When is all of this damn nightmare going to be over? Not parts and pieces, but the whole thing, done. I just want to wake up at home beside you and know everything might be okay again. How do we keep living freely and stress-free after all of this is done? I know it can't last forever, but when does it end? That's the question. I'm thinking if they keep me in county it would probably be only if I waive the appeal. At least that sounds like something they would say. I know I've got high hopes of not having to go to prison. I need to just accept the fact I'm no one's favorite, and they are going to screw me one last time while they can. God forbid if I catch a break and something goes right for me.

I'm mentally exhausted and am tired of wondering and worrying about what may or may not happen. Why don't they just do whatever it is they're going to do and get it over with? This is mental torture. When you get home got to the grocery store and get some sushi, then go fishing at the dock, that should get you feeling better, lol... I'm sure you will get back on food stamps. Are you going to stay with dad till I get out or are you going to try to find us a place I can be at? I don't know where I can't and can be or who or what I can be around. Will you get a hold of Tennessee and ask about the laws on it there are? Also, ask them if there are any programs or anything to help me get housing and a job with my charge, in case I don't get an appeal. I love and miss you, honey, and I'm over it all together.

How does Brown go from telling me no more than two years to telling me now two-four years? Am I being punished even more for using my right to a trial and didn't win? I don't think I'm being treated fairly and haven't been since I got here. I want to just get a fair deal like I deserve. I don't have a bad record; why am I going to prison when everyone that lives around here get multiple felonies and go home? If I don't get an appeal, this will be my first felony. I just don't understand it. First, they don't or won't reduce my bond; okay I get that I don't live here. But why send me to prison on my first felony from a fucked up hear-say case? The jury was made well aware I don't live here; everything that was used against me in this case didn't have anything to do with it. My kids, child support, my prior DV's, where I live, and my work history had nothing to do with it, and shouldn't have been able to be brought up or used since I wasn't allowed to use my markings, the polygraph, or let them know I was incarcerated for seven months. It's easy to see I wasn't treated fair and should've either got a mistrial or found not guilty on a hearsay case and no evidence. When Smith mentioned me as an inbred sperm donor, the judge just let the jury laugh. What is wrong with these people? Low oxygen? I want to be back in TN ASAP, where this county or state has no more control of me. Am I the only one that sees I'm getting railroaded? If other legal figures see and are aware that I am, then why won't anyone help me get this overturned, so I can go home and continue a normal life? Hell, even the judge should see I've been given an unfair verdict based on hearsay and things that didn't have anything to do with the case and overturn it. Brown should've objected to a lot more but the judge being for Smith; he would've let it go anyhow. Well, I'm going to get this shit day over. I love you and Happy Easter.

Love Always & forever, Amen
Jimmy


April 22, 2017

Hello, Dear,

How are you today? I'm okay, I guess. I'm just sitting here, wanting to get to court, so I can get all this shit done and behind me. I'm sick of being in here; same thing in the same cage, day after day with the same people, and I tell ya it got old a long time ago, so now I sit and keep to myself as much as possible and pray time goes fast. I love and miss you, Ria. I'm sorry I'm not with you to fix the car and things. I'm having a really bad day; it seems everything is bothering me and getting on my nerves. It's one of those days where I grit my teeth and try to sleep it away.

I do believe I am done with this place, state, and everything and everyone in it. I'm not here trying to make friends. I don't want any. I'm ready to go home and away from this ignorant, selfish, childish-ass people. I've got patience, but after eight months, it's thin. Why the fuck doesn't anyone know how to install a headlight? Honey, I'm over everything. Why do they have to drag out all the court dates here? Since this was more or less an open and shut case, then it should've been done and me sentenced months ago. Then I can finally do whatever I got to do and get it over for good.

You should've already be back in TN; this whole car deal wouldn't have happened. Don't worry about coming to visit until you get the headlight fixed. It's dark when you leave here, and it would be unsafe, and I don't want you stuck driving at night. It would be different if it was the passenger side. I tell ya, since we've been here it's been one thing after another. Maybe once we get back south, our luck and life will go back to normal. I hope they give me probation and let me go home, but I guess I'll know what the P.O. is going to recommend soon. I wish the judge would overturn this, but I know he's all for Smith. You know there are so many ways it could go at court for sentencing, and all we can do is hope for the best.

Baby you are so cute, and it's the little things you do that make me love you and make me laugh. I was all stressed out, thinking the headlight was all smashed up and didn't work at all, and now you tell me the LED's and the high beam work, and it's just the low beam that doesn't work and the outer part of the headlight is broke. So, here's what I say to you, lol...replace the bulb and tape the outside of the headlight, ya DINK!!! LMAO. I love you, it's goofy little things you do that make me smile and miss you even more.

Believe me, as much as I pray, I can't wait to be back with

you. The headlight should be fine till you get back to TN or until I can get out to fix it. This county pretty much does what they want. They pick and choose who to keep in county and who to throw away. I'm stressed beyond my means over all of this, but I know it can't last forever. It already feels like forever since we was happy together. Twenty-four days till court again. I'm going to ask the P.O. if she could just recommend five years' probation, so I can go home. I don't get in trouble, so I should be okay, plus I don't have a violent history, except for the couple of DVs, but I guess it's up to her, Smith, and the judge. I'm interested in what all Brown will have to say, if anything, to get this overturned and/or a minimum sentence.

I don't know or see how our life is ever going to be normal if I don't get the judge to see through her lies or I get it done by appeal. Have you checked to see if there is any programs or organizations to help people with CSC charges get housing or a job? Why are these fucking people so anxious to send me to prison on a bullshit accusation charge with no proof and it being eight years old? Do you know if this is considered a violent charge? Well, goodnight honey. I love you.


April 23, 2017


Good morning, honey,


I love and miss you. Well, today is race day, and they are racing in Bristol, TN.; imagine that. We need to go see that race one day. I've actually gotten into NASCAR. I'm not really trying to think too far ahead of what we can or can't do or look forward to until after sentencing. Every time I get my hopes up or think something will change, I get let down. I don't see how they could take my life from me with no evidence and how did it happen in one day? What kind of trial lasts only one day? They didn't give the jury time to think or consider anything. The judge wasn't going to let them leave until a verdict was made, and I think they were being pressured since they seemed to be tired and they wanted to go home. Why anybody don't see this was an unjust, bias trial and won't help me is baffling. So, you started your book, huh? How's that going so far? I'm sure Brown could suggest tips or someone to help you with it or getting it published, seeing he has a book of his own out.

Have you heard from housing in TN since you returned the app? What are we going to do when I get out? You know housing isn't going to let me live there. Life is so fucked up. Why can't I find help? It's so plain to see I didn't do any of what she is accusing. None of her stories match up or made sense. I was an easy target, and they knew it. There was so much Brown could've done to prove my innocence, but didn't. Why? Why was Smith allowed to use Rose's counseling, but we couldn't? Then they used child support and not working against me, How? They had no case, no proof, no nothing. Why didn't the judge see that? And from eight years ago, come on...I'm no lawyer or judge, but it's plain to see I got railroaded. Isn't there any organizations or pro-bono people or anyone that's willing to see through this county's shit and help me? We need someone outside of this county; it seems everyone here is for their own, regardless of proof.

There's got to be someone; even a few of the guards I've been talking to since I've been here, couldn't believe it. One even said she was keeping up with it and said she was sorry and when the verdict came back; all she could say was, "Oh, jeez." I have a lot of folks in here that think I should've won my case. I didn't get to spend any days or enough time with the jury to express my opinions or my story with them to show my innocence. I'm so angry, frustrated, and upset. After all of this has happened to me, it makes me ask myself and wonder: How many people are sitting in prison with false accusations? When I get out, I'm thinking about doing a lot of research and dedicate my free time trying to help or sponsor wrongfully accused people around our community. Why is it "we the people" are expected to follow the laws but the system or the "higher citizens" don't have to? It was easy to see there was no case, but I guess her testimony was coached to please the judge, Smith, and the jury, so it didn't matter about my defense; it isn't fair and unjust. Do you think if you brought all of this to the newspaper they would get involved in trying to help me?

Something needs to be done to expose the way they do things here. But just because I'm charged "for now" with this, isn't going to stop me from believing in humanity and the truth. The news and papers should eat up the fact I was accused and convicted without evidence, an investigation and the fact it being eight years ago and when her mom wants full custody of our girls. Personally, I don't think I stood a chance since day one. It was a made-up story with nothing to go on except Rose's mouth. How can they get away with convicting me of this based on her story, a picture of a house, a pic of her when she was six, my two DVs, me not paying child support, and not working the last seven months? That stuff had nothing to do with the case and all of that was the whole case. In other words, there wasn't one, and Rias even said he didn't do or look into anything. There was too many flags and holes in this case to see I was innocent; I just don't get it. Are they stupid or just retarded to not care that I got screwed?

The judge encouraged the jury to come to a verdict instead of giving them the copy of Rose's testimony, like they wanted. What he should've done was call it a day, then have the court reporter type up the transcript, so they had it available the next morning, instead of pushing and pressuring them to do it all in one day. I really think the judge is a part of me just getting pushed through the system. That is why I don't think he will overturn it and step on the feet of the "good ole' boys club." If I had money or knew someone who would take it on, I'd sue the shit out of this county. We need a pro-bono Erin Brockovich...lol. If this crooked ass county is really going to convict me on a "make believe trial," then they should at least give me county time and not prison. I'm sure the judge knows I'm going to appeal this. I'm just hoping the appellant lawyers and judges have nothing to do with or know anyone in or from this county.

You know what I find as a flag, that her story was made up, when she said we climbed into my blue jeans together. Well, I don't wear baggy clothes and wore a size thirty-two in the waist. How could anyone believe that to even be possible? There was so many flags and inconsistences to her story, and Smith kept insisting no proof and evidence is or was needed to back her story. Well, why not? Cause they didn't care about my side to begin with. Why didn't Brown object to him using stuff that didn't pertain to the case, like my kids, work, and child support? All of these things I think about daily. I've noticed that Brown changed his stories up to. He said if we could get at least one person to say not guilty, we'd be okay. Then the judge said they (the jury) have to agree before they could leave. This whole case was done wrongfully, and they still aren't done yet. I really don't trust anyone in the system here, including Smith and the judge. They are both fairly new and making a name for themselves quick. They are both prison happy and go hand in hand. I wonder what Brown, the judge, and Smith were talking about so long in the judge's chambers, when they was waiting on the verdict and we was in the court room? They were in there ten-fifteen minutes. Can we say conspiracy!!!!

Well my head hurts, so I will write again soon.

Love always, your husband,
Jimmy

April 23, 2017

Hello, baby,

I love and miss you very much. I have starting writing that book on Saturday. I just woke up and started writing and haven't stopped but long enough to piss, smoke a cig, and get something to eat; that's if I remember to do so, then it's back to writing. I am now up to page forty-three, and there's still more to write, and then there is our letters that have to be included.

I have changed some names, so I don't get sued if this book ever does get published, but places, times, dates, and events are staying original. That would be cool if my book about our lives was sitting on book shelves at Barnes & Noble, Books-A-Million and anywhere else books are sold. Maybe, just maybe, our book will help someone else that has been falsely accused, dragged through the mud, and had their names slandered over lies and false accusations.

Three weeks from Tuesday, and we will find out if you get to come home or not. I really hope and pray that the judge does the right thing and releases you, so we can pack up the car and blow this popsicle stand because I don't like the flavors that they have been serving up!! lol.

I am so ready to go back to Tennessee with you and get back to some kind of normal life; whatever that is anymore. I know it will take a while to rebuild our lives, but as long as we are together, we can do it!! If you do get to come home, the first night we are together, all I want to do is lay in bed and hold you and talk all night (sex is optional...lol). I just want us to be whole again. I know I get to talk to you every day, but it's not the same as when we just hold each other and talk about everything. I MISS US!!!!!

This book I am writing starts when we first met at Se-lena's to the present. I have left some things out because I didn't think the world needed to know certain things that should remain private. I have kept it as accurate as possible with dates and events in our lives. I want you to read it before I try to get it published.

I was debating if I should include all of the songs and poems that I wrote for you, but for the songs, I would probably have to have permission from the artists to be able to include them in our book. The poems I probably could, but I'm not sure about the songs. I want to include pictures, as well. What do you think? This book is not just about this case, but it's about you, me, and us and some things that we have been through since we met. So, I need your opinion and some ideas about the story of our lives.

I love you baby, and I miss your arms wrapped around me at night and hearing your heartbeat and falling asleep to it. The days are long and empty, but the nights are even worse without you beside me keeping me safe and protected. I want everything back that we have lost or missed out on, but I know that won't ever happen, and I am trying to deal with it as best as I can, but it still hurts.

I am going to end this letter but will write again after our visit on Tuesday, I can't wait to see you, baby!!!!

Loving You Forever,
Your One and Only Wife,
Ri-Ri

May 4, 2017

Hello, honey,

Well, we have got a week and a half till sentencing, so I figured I'd write one last letter from here. I love you and miss you very much. I don't know what's going to happen or where I'll be in a couple weeks. I want to thank you for having hope and staying positive, but I'm sure we both know what's going to happen, since the judge has been against me and on Smith's side since I arrived here. Everything we didn't think would happen, has and what we thought would, didn't, so why have hope the judge will overturn this? I am hoping though that the PO will see I got railroaded on a bullshit case and maybe try to help me by either recommending an acquittal or time served with probation, or county or something, but like I said, this system is corrupt, so I really don't look forward too much and if Brown was going to help me in any way, he would've at trial. He did what we thought he would...the minimum. With luck and hope, maybe the appellant lawyer will do what Brown couldn't or didn't want to do. I just hope it doesn't take years.

Please don't stop trying to find someone to help me. I've never felt so helpless and thrown away in my life; it's a very awful feeling. No matter what happens, just remember I love you, and please stay in Tennessee and take care of Dad. It has been a long nine months, and I think my gray hair has tripled. Well, what little is growing back. My fuckin' knee hurts, and I'm just tired if all of this and everything involved in this county. They let all these thieves, meth-heads and repeat offenders with multiple twenty-year felonies off with six to twelve months in county and probation, and I got a fifteen-year felony with no priors and a few misdemeanors, and they are sending me under the jail. Just doesn't make sense. If God loves me even a smidgen, now would be a good time to show it and whisper in the judge's ear for me.

Well, honey, I'm going to end this letter. I might write one more, but I guess that would be it till you get back to TN. I love you now and forever, honey.

Love Always and forever, Amen
Your Husband, Jimmy

# CHAPTER 6: Sentencing

The trial in itself was exhausting, and it took an emotional toll on both Jimmy and me. We were both still in shock that he was found guilty. A week after the trial sentencing was scheduled for the next month, May 6. So, for a little over a month, we were both scared of what kind of time he would get. I was feeling guilty for a long time because I kept telling Jimmy not to take any plea deal that the prosecution was offering.

We had discussed many times the possibility of him going to prison, but I was still hoping that the judge would reverse the verdict and let Jimmy come home where he belongs. But with the way everything has gone against him, we knew he wouldn't be coming home any time soon. I continued to go see Jimmy at the jail every Tuesday, and we still wrote our letters and talked on the phone every day. We were both trying to stay strong and positive for each other, but deep down we were both scared as hell of what was to happen in May.

There was a tough decision that I had to make and that was when do I go back to Tennessee. Well, that decision was made for me after the hearing. I talked to Tony and Ann after the hearing, and we all thought it would be best for everyone that I left right after sentencing because none of us trusted Kathy and what she might do next. The closer May 16 got, the higher my anxiety level would go and the scarier it became for Jimmy. Neither one of us were sleeping very well, and the days just seemed to drag on and on. We were both very frightened because if he was sent to prison, we both know and have heard the stories of what happens to people that have the same charges as Jimmy.

The possibility of Jimmy getting hurt, or even worse, while he's in prison had me fearful and scared that I may never see him again.

The weekend before sentencing, I started getting my car packed with just about everything I had brought up from Tennessee in November 2016. Believe me, I even amazed myself how well I packed the car...Jimmy would be proud! There were a couple of things that wouldn't fit, but they can be replaced. The day before sentencing was very stressful, and my anxiety level was up once again, and Jimmy was a nervous wreck, and I was worried about his blood pressure going up through all the stress he was under.

Tuesday, May 16 was here, and I finished packing the car with my pillows and blankets, I said my goodbyes to Ann and Tony, and I left for the courthouse. Court was supposed to start at 3:00 P.M, but it didn't start until 3:45 P.M. Mr. Brown first filed a motion for a full acquittal of the guilty plea because during the trial the prosecutor "opened the door" to Rose's counseling and for the lack of evidence. But just like everything else, it, too, was denied. I was not allowed to read my character witness statement in court, but Kathy and Rose's victim impact statements were read in court.

Rose's was ridiculous because she used words in it that she either had to have a dictionary or she had someone tell her what to write, like an adult coaching her. Kathy's was even worse; she stated that she wished Jimmy would spend the rest of his life in prison and that she knew there some of Jimmy's family members were in town to support him and that she was afraid of their vindictive wrath for sending Jimmy to prison. OKAY...WHATEVER! That really pissed me off because for one, I was the only one in town for Jimmy and two, she was the one that was being vindictive, driving by the house I was staying at, flipping me off for no reason, and attacking me and the people I was staying with on Facebook, posting all kinds of stupid shit, along with the false accusations, slander, and lies.

The probation officer had done a presentencing investigation to see where Jimmy fell in on the sentencing guidelines. Her recommendation was twelve to twenty-four months, the prosecutor was pushing for six years, but the judge went against both of them and went outside the guidelines and gave Jimmy thirty-six months in prison. Now, remember, Jimmy was only charged with two counts: one he was acquitted for, the second he found guilty, but the says his reasoning for the thirty-six months was because, according to Rose, he should have been charged with four counts of CSC 2nd for supposedly touching four different times…such bullshit!

Like I said before, this county picks and chooses who they want to send to prison. Jimmy was even offered a deal before sentencing, that if he didn't file for an appeal that he would get a county cap; sounded fishy to me. I was allowed to hug and kiss Jimmy after court, and we knew that was going to be the last time we saw each other for God knows how long. He was going to be transferred to Marquette the next morning, and I left to go back to Tennessee after court. I hated having to leave him in Michigan, but he wanted me to go home and help take care of Big Jimmy, and he knew that I didn't have any where to stay in Michigan; he wanted me as far away from Kathy, as well.

Before I left, I had to go over to the jail and pick up all of Jimmy's personal effects, letters, clothes, and anything else he had because he couldn't take anything with him when he gets transferred but a piece of paper with names, addresses, and phone numbers on it. I left and started my long journey back home. It was about 5:00 P.M. when I got on the highway, and Jimmy would call me every half hour to every hour just to see how I was doing and how far I was. This went on until 4:15 AM. on Wednesday, and that was the last phone call I got from Jimmy because he was leaving for Marquette at 7:00 A.M., and he had no more money for phone calls.

# CHAPTER 7: After Sentencing

May 17, 2017 was the day that began one of three transfers for Jimmy to three different prisons. The first was to the prison in Marquette, Michigan, known as a quarantine stop. He was there from May 17 to May 23, where he was transferred again to Jackson, Michigan. That prison he was processed through the Department of Corrections. Jimmy was there for roughly thirty days, and he wouldn't know where he was going next until the night before his move.

During his time in Jackson, I finally got a phone call from him on Saturday, June 10, at 8:45 in the morning. It had been three weeks since we had talked on the phone, and it drove me crazy not being able to hear his voice. That Saturday was the first day that he was able to start making phone calls, and he had just started receiving mail two days before that. I must have called the prison in Jackson at least six times, trying to find out if he was okay, when he could make calls and receive mail. The officials were telling me yes to all my questions, but come to find out from Jimmy that he wasn't able to do anything or get any mail until he was done going through processing.

I was so relieved when he did call me, at least I knew he was okay and nothing had happened to him. Jimmy told me that there were twenty phones outside and about three hundred inmates, so basically, it's first come, first served or they had to stand in line to use the phones. He also told me that they only go outside about two-three times a week for forty minutes, so I wouldn't hear from him every, day but he would call as often as he could.

Jimmy was in Jackson for about two weeks, when he was transferred yet again to a prison in Adrian, Michigan. This was his last and final place where he would serve out the rest of his thirty-six-month sentence. Right before he was moved, he was assigned an appellant lawyer out of Lansing, Michigan. I spoke to this attorney, and he told me that he has to get all of the records, transcripts, and Jimmy's file from his previous lawyer and talk to Jimmy first before he would even speak to me about the case.

So, that's where we are right now...waiting for the appeal process to start, and hopefully we will be able to get his sentence overturned and he be able to come home to Tennessee, where he belongs. The lies, false accusations, shoddy police investigation and unfair treatment in the judicial system has put Jimmy where he is today. The next four letters are from Jimmy, when he was in Marquette and Jackson, but since he has been in Adrian, I haven't received any more letters because we are able to talk on the phone, the sound of his voice gives me some comfort to know that he is doing as well as can be expected in his current situation.

HOME IS WHERE HE BELONGS....NOT IN PRISON!!!!!!

May 17, 2017

Ria,

Hi, honey...well, I'm in Marquette right now, and I'm missing you so much. I love you, and I'm hoping time goes by quick. I'm just in holding right now. When I got here I changed out, seen a mental health worker, and a nurse for meds and got a TB shot. I told them about my knee, but I'm not sure what's going to happen. They said I'll probably be sent down to Jackson next Monday or Wednesday. From what I hear so far is once I'm there it should be about two-three weeks before I get where I'm going. I hope you got back to Dad's okay. My inmate # 361179; you have to use it for everything you or I do.

I really hope my appeal can get this overturned or a sentence reduction. The guy in the cell next to me said he has been here a week and a half. He said he got his appeal paperwork today; he said it took eight days. So, hopefully, I'll know who my attorney is soon. My main goal is to stay to myself and try to get a job or into a trade to take up most of my time. Here there's nothing to do but sit, read, or write letters. They do have a radio on, though. I can't wait to hear from you; write as much as possible. Your letters are all I've got to look forward to. I'm lost, scared, and alone. I just wish I could hear your voice, but they took that away, too.

I'm not even where I'm going or in general population yet, and already anxiety is kicking in. It's going to be a long two-year, four-month nightmare that even counseling won't help me recover from. If there is a hell, I'm in it. Why did God abandon me? Not that I have much faith in God, but why? God, get me through this with no problems. My worst fear is getting stabbed or beat to death. I'm not a big guy, and I'm not sure if I'll make it two years.

Ria, honey, I love and miss our life so much. Will we ever be happy and normal again? Baby, there isn't anything I can do to help myself in here. What's even worse is I can't do anything to help and watch after you; you depending on me as a spouse, not only financially, but physically, emotionally, and for security and for me to always be there for you, and I've utterly failed you. When you needed me the most, I can't be there. Please, know one way or another I will make it up to you. I guess I'm going to go for now, but not forever.

I love and miss you so much. Tell Dad and Rosalie I love them, and I'll write again soon.

Loving you always and forever, amen
Your Husband, Jimmy

May 25, 2017

Ria,

Hey, love, how are ya doing? I finally made it here to Jackson. I guess I'll be here about three-four weeks. Have you got any new or good news? How's my dad been? I've gotten no mail, so I don't know much. I see a nurse for my meds, and she said I should qualify for the boot camp program, and I should talk to a counselor about it next week, about Wednesday, since this Monday is a holiday.

I love and miss you!! I tell ya, this is a totally new world and experience. I was in a one-man cell the first night, and today I got moved in another cell today with a bunkie. I'm tired of being moved around from facility to facility and cell to cell. After three-four weeks, I'll be classified, and I'll be moved to a different prison again!! Hopefully, I'll get in the program. I guess that's all anybody in here has is hope. As you can tell, they don't have or give us paper, so we got to find and make do with what we can.

Since I haven't heard anything, I really don't have a lot to talk about, but I'm trying. Did you get into housing or anything yet? How's Dad's health? I hope you write me soon, so I know what's going on. I still haven't heard from the lawyer yet, so I hope they turned the paperwork in. I suppose I'm doing best to be expected, although I'm nowhere near being done or getting out. I'll know more next week or so.

I miss the sound of your voice and seeing your smile. What have you been doing to pass the time? Fishing yet? Or the flea market? It sucks, but we will get through this. Where did you store all of our stuff? Yesterday and today, I at least got outside for about forty-five minutes. It feels good to get some fresh air. I was reading the prison handbook, and I guess at the end of the minimum thirty-six-month sentence, I'm eligible for parole but not guaranteed to get it. They can keep denying me all the way to the max of fifteen years.

How's the kids and grands? Did dad get his prosthetic nose yet? Please write me. I've been waiting for a letter, and I don't know when I'll be able to call. Hell, I don't even know if you've put money on my books. At least I'm writing in pen, but it's one of the stupid flex pens. I love and miss you. Have you been doing okay for the most part? I hope the car is still okay. I really don't have much to write about, but I'll keep in touch as much as possible.

Write me and let me know if you've heard anything new and let me know how you are doing. I hope you haven't changed your mind and gave up on me. I know that was a stupid thought. I know you won't. I'll let you know as soon as I hear from the appellant lawyer. I'm hoping, maybe you have heard something, cause I haven't heard nothing from no one. Did you do anything for Memorial Day?

Well, I'm hoping to start getting letters and hearing news this week. I love and miss you, honey. It already feels like forever, which sucks since I'm only a week or so into it. I tell ya, this place is a fucking nightmare. I can guarantee this shit will never happen again…if I make it out of this shit to begin with. I should only be here another three weeks. Then off to where ever. They only give us one envelope to write home while we are here, but if I can scrounge another one up, then I'll try to write again in a week or so.

I love you very much. Tell dad I love him, too.

Love Always & Forever, Amen,
Jimmy

June 3, 2017

Hello, beautiful,

I got your letters today! Unfortunately, I still haven't been able to use the phone yet. I love and miss you so much. I still haven't heard from the appellant attorney or anyone from the boot camp program. I'm still going through the orientation process, so that might be why. And, yes, honey, get you a cat!! LOL That would be good if you get a regular apartment, but just remember I can't be there. But I guess I'll worry about it when it comes up. I'm glad Dad and Rosalie are doing okay. I've been doing what I can to stay busy, reading, sleeping, and writing you. I'm doing okay so far, so don't worry so much.

Since I got sentenced it seems like forever already. Have you found out if my appeal papers were even turned into the courts and filed? I've got a feeling they may have gotten lost or misplaced, if you know what I mean. I gave them to the guard after I filled them out, and she said she would put them in the court box. I just hope Rias didn't get ahold of them and trash them. I think I've only got forty-two days to file for an appeal, so please make sure they were filed.

This place is quarantine/orientation, and they have some of the worst criminals coming through here. If you can think of it, it's here. There's an ass load of young folks from eighteen to twenty-five years old. Most are here for their first time; there's a lot of murderers and CSC's offenders. Some folks here seem to not understand the severity of what their charges could do or cause them. The guy in the cell next to me is doing a minimum of ten years for 2- CSC 1st and 1 CSC 2nd degree and doesn't seem to care who knows. There was one black guy who finished up here and got transferred to a Level 5 max prison, serving two, yes, two natural life sentences for killing seven people. He will never see the light of day again. There is an India or Pakistani guy here for acts of terrorism and serving forty-six yrs.

The guy I'm currently sharing a cell with is a fifty-year-old biker; he is here for one year and two months for his third DUI...so, yep, there's a little of everything here, and then there's me. I'm here for twenty-seven months for "possession by association of Meth," at which I'm currently appealing. But on that note here is the downfall, at the end of orientation you get a copy of your PSI...which is the presentencing investigation and other papers you have to have for intake where I'm going next. So, my plan is to split it up in different envelopes and send it to you once I get where I'm going. It will include what level I am, where I'm at, full criminal report, including word for word why or how I got my current charge and my early release date.

I'm sure I'll be a Level 1, and the shitty part is no one is guaranteed parole at the end of their minimum sentence, as I found out so no they don't have to release me at the end of the twenty-seven months. I know it's B/S, right? I believe I'll be okay, though; I follow the rules and don't put myself in a position to get involved in any trouble. I'm hoping and praying for the appeal to come along and this get overturned. That is really my only hope of peace and serenity. I know there are people in here for a lot longer than me, but if I have to do the full twenty-seven months, then I'm sure it's going to feel like eternity.

I hope when I'm eligible for parole they let me return to TN and don't try to keep me here. It says in the handbook: "Parole to another state is possible if the other state agrees to accept supervision and if any restitution ordered by the court is paid in full." It also says: "At a minimum the prisoner should provide a second choice of home placement in case the first choice is disapproved or not available at the time of parole." And for prisoners not serving a sentence of life, parole terms ordered by the parole board may be six months, twelve months, fifteen, eighteen, twenty-four, or the sentencing max date, which in my case is fifteen years. Then it says parole is not guaranteed, parole is not assured for any prisoner, there's no guarantee of parole based merely on technical eligibility for release prior to the expiration of the maximum term.

So, who knows when I'll be out or back in TN; once I get out, I hope they don't keep me in this state until parole is done. You should be able to go on the Michigan.gov website and get all the parole info. I love and miss you, and, yes, it's crazy talk for you to think I'd forget about or stop writing you!! Once I get to the other place you can order care packs and a secure pack of food and stuff, and also hygiene. You can order those on my behalf, and they will ship it to where I'm at. You'll have to call the prison or here and ask about it and for the website. I think the secure pack of food is $85, and the website is securepack.com (I think).

So far, I'm staying clear of B/S and just taking it day by day. They offer jobs and trade classes, so you can have a certified trade when we get out. I'm thinking about auto mechanic or welding. Did you get any of my letters I sent you from Marquette? I sent out three. How is your book coming along? I worry how you're doing. Please write as much as possible. Today you said in your letter that you hope your last letter reached me. Well, I received two from you today and that's it, so if you wrote me while I was in Marquette, then I never got it. Like I said except for the two letters today, I've heard nothing from no one...it's as if I don't exist.

If I get an appeal and get this overturned or when I get parole, are you going to pick me up from where ever I am, or do I need to make arrangements to get at least to Knoxville, if I'm able to parole to TN? Well, I think Crossville would be closer. I'd feel a lot better if I could at least get a letter from the appellant lawyer. I hope he or she sees right away that I got railroaded, but it'll be at least fourteen to sixteen months to get an appeal heard. So, it'll be around July or August 2018. Shit, by then I'll have six months left. I got screwed in a county where they are for each other instead of for justice, and I'm going to make it well known once I get out.

Have you tried the Attorney General again since I didn't get a change of venue, plus he exceeded past my recommended guidelines of twelve to twenty-four months? My whole trial was B/S and unfair. There's got to be somebody who can help with the corruption of the county and my case.

I'll write again soon, and I love and miss you so much and Dad, too!!! Please write back ASAP.

Loving You Always,
Jimmy


June 7, 2017

Hello, honey,

I love and miss you so much!! I got your card with the Facebook joke in it. I still haven't heard anything from a lawyer. Please call and make sure it got filed. I've only got forty-two days to file an appeal, and it's been three weeks, and so far, nothing. I have a feeling it didn't get filed. Also, I'm not eligible for the boot camp program. I got classified as a Level 1, so telling where I'll be. I'm sending a sheet that was given to me here, saying they amended the law that the judge has me sentenced under, MCL 750 code...I'm required on top of everything else to Lifetime Electronic Monitoring(GPS)...I mean, WTF?

Ria, they are doing everything against me. Two things have to happen: find out if my appeal is filed and I have a lawyer, or get me one now!!! Time is running out, I'm so done and over this shit. My early release date is Sept. 1, 2019. The couple of letters I've gotten from you have been short; are you okay? Can you get ahold of those people in Ohio and see what the price is for appeal help? I'm stuck, scared, and don't know what to do. Well, I can't do anything in here.

I'm relying solely on you to find out about everything. Tell Dad and Rosalie I love and miss them, too. All I know is the parole board is strict, and I'm here thirty-six months (minimum) to fifteen years (max), unless it's overturned by appeal. So, what now? I'm on the verge of just giving up and just sit till they decide to let me go. I don't want to give up, but after forty-two days, my appeal is fucked, and all hope would be lost. Please keep trying to find me help.

I miss your voice. I'll call as soon as I can. I got a receipt where you put $53 on my books; I've got $47 left because they charged me $5 for a padlock for my locker. Did you pay my fine and fee? I wish we could just get back to our life, but I've got a feeling it's going to be a long, long time. I feel so helpless. How did Dad's appointment go? Everything okay? I'll try to keep in touch as much as possible. I just pray I get an appellant lawyer and I make it out of this nightmare okay.

Remember, no matter what, I love and miss ya'll very much. Please find out or do as much as you can to find out about the appeal and let me know.

Love Always & Forever ~ Amen ~
Your Husband, Jimmy

# About the Authors

Maria Moeller-Hackler was born on January 6, 1968, in Albany, Georgia. She was adopted by a loving family. Her father was a Marine, and her mother was a nurse. Maria was the youngest of six, five of whom were adopted, including herself.

She grew up in North Charleston, South Carolina, where she went to elementary, middle, and high school. She later moved to Florence, South Carolina, for a few years. In 1991, she gave birth to her daughter, Jessica, and in 1994, she had a son, Andrew. Then in 1995, she met Jimmy, and the rest is history. She now resides in Tennessee. Both of her children are grown, and she has four, beautiful grandchildren.

James V. Hackler III was born in Charleston, South Carolina, on December 27, 1977. He went to elementary, middle, and high school in Charleston. He met his first wife, and they had three children together, but they divorced just six years later. Jimmy also served in the Army, then he became a long-haul truck driver until 2011.

In 2013, Jimmy and Maria were reunited after years apart. They were married on September 4, 2019, proving that no matter how long it takes to be together, "If it's meant to be, it will happen."

Their battle for justice and for Jimmy's freedom is ongoing.

Class of
2013

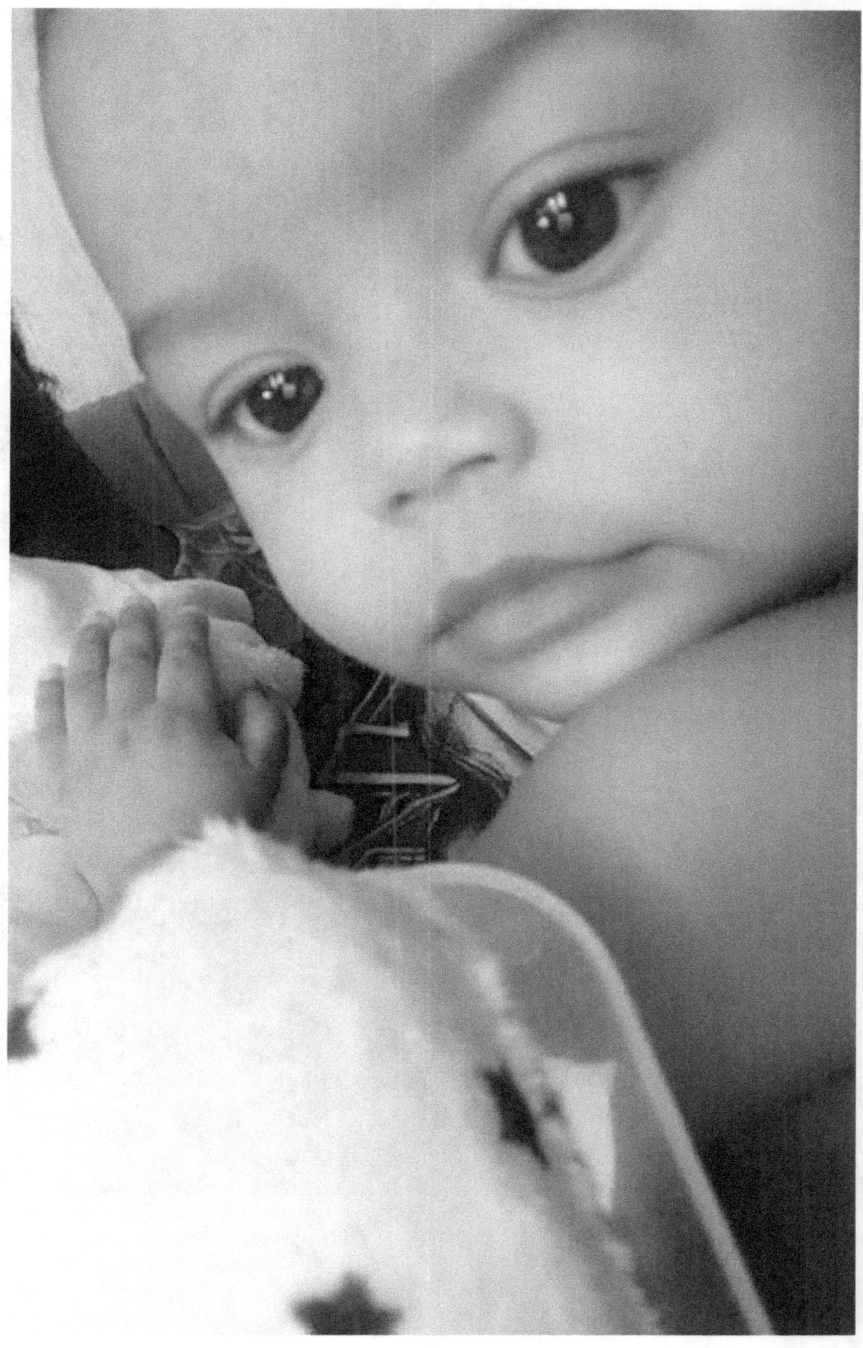